Can't Tell Me Nothing:

The Uncomfortable Hair Truths of Black Women

Presented by

Dr. Carey Yazeed

Shero Books

Subsidiary of Shero Productions, L.L.C.

Louisiana

Shero Books, a subsidiary of Shero Productions, LLC., P.O. Box 2405, Gonzales, LA. 70707

Can't Tell Me Nothing: The Uncomfortable Hair Truths of Black Women

For information on the book or to contact any of the contributing authors for signings, interviews, and other events visit: www.canttellmenothingbook.com or email: drcareyyazeed@gmail.com

ISBN: 978-0-9850316-5-7
Printed in the United States of America

Table of Contents

"The hair is the richest ornament of women"
~ Martin Luther King Jr.

Introduction

airstyles have always been an essential part of Black culture. During slavery, braids were used in various ways as a source of survival. Depending on the style, braids hid rice that could be cooked and eaten when food was sparse and they served as maps with routes to freedom for runaways. We all know how songs were used to articulate for those wanting to escape, but did you know that certain hairstyles on female slaves were used for the same purposes?

Our hair and the styles that we wear are more than just "a look." Yes, they represent something much more profound. Black hair reveals how we are feeling and what we have experienced. Black hair serves as more than just a regal crown. Our hair reminds us to stand tall and hold our heads high as we face a new day of uncertainty in a world that still has difficulty accepting us for who we are.

Black hair can tell you what our goals are in life, what we aspire to achieve, and our various accomplishments. Sometimes, if you look closely enough, you can even tell if a Black woman is experiencing health issues like anxiety, cancer, or malnutrition by merely looking at her hair.

But there are some things that our hair doesn't tell you. It doesn't tell you about our unspoken pains, like discrimination in the workplace because we wear locs. Our hair can not express that we feel unaccepted or unloved by our significant others because they do not like our hair's texture. Our hair doesn't indicate the harmful messages that have been ingrained in little Black girls, with chemical relaxers and curl enhancers like the Jheri Curl. You can't look at our hair and know that deep down some of us feel that we aren't pretty enough and our hair doesn't look white enough. You'd never know from looking at our hairstyles that Black women believe that to be accepted, we must alter the natural state of our hair over and over again; changing who we naturally are just to fit in and feel like we belong.

With the spoken joys and recent embrace of natural hair in the Black community come just as many unspoken truths and traumas that Black women endure because of their hair. We endure the self-hate mixed messages, the bullying by other Black women because we love to wear our hair straight or enhance it with weaves and extensions. Our unspoken truths have been so painful and harmful that Representative Cedric Richmond of New Orleans, Louisiana introduced the CROWN Act (Creating a Respectful and Open World for Natural Hair) of 2020. The CROWN Act, if passed by the Senate, will prohibit discrimination based on a person's hair texture or hairstyle, mainly if it is commonly associated with a particular race or national origin. Yes, in 2021, we still require the passage of laws to protect us and our hair.

Can't Tell Me Nothing is a critical anthology that helps us to talk about things that hurt when it comes to Black hair; what makes us uncomfortable and squeamish with pain as we recall our personal history with hair care from the kitchen to the salon. Sixteen brave Black women have poured out their souls in this book. They share about their unspoken pains and hair traumas; the things we don't like to talk about when it comes to Black hair, but they impact us just the same. My hope is that this anthology will serve as a guide, helping Black women to become comfortable in their truths when it comes to their hair. My aspirations are for us to embrace our hair freedom and, with it, learn how to boldly embrace who we are when it comes to setting trends, defending our crowns, and unapologetically taking in all of who God meant for us to be, hair and all.

Dr. Carey Yazeed

The Hair Game

Edwina

*E*veryone wants to be successful, but unfortunately, there are rules to this game, especially for a Black woman. If you're going to win in Corporate America (public or private), you have to play their game. This game is whatever the rule-makers perceive it to be. If you want to get in, you have to learn how to play well.

MOMENT OF TRUTH

I am a Black female living in the South, and I was raised to act and behave a certain way. I watched these behaviors manifest in other women, and so I came to expect the same things for myself. In a nutshell, Black women have to look and act a certain way if we want to be accepted in mainstream America. We have to follow the rules and follow a specific path; education, grooming, etc., and hair is a big part. We can call it the Hair Game.

When I walk through the doors of Corporate America, I must wear the uniform: business suits and conservative dresses. They are the ones who determine whether you fit in or you sit on the sidelines. My hair is one of the most significant determining factors; straight hair, long hair, conservative hair. It fits perfectly with the uniform. We always have to look friendly and easy on the eyes because kinks, tight curls, and afros are threatening to the game makers.

I quickly learned if I wanted to be a "successful Black woman," I would have to learn how to play my part. In my twenties, it was the perms. Everyone I knew would make sure their hair was straight and permed, no matter if it was a short or long style.

I remember I decided to be different and go a little longer before I got my next perm. I was quickly reprimanded by one of my friends (another Black woman). She carefully informed me that my perm was long overdue, and I should immediately handle that! I had to be "straight" and "stay straight" to be accepted.

As a result of this, I associated a new perm with my self-worth. If I had a fresh perm, then I was beautiful, and they would accept me to play in their "hair games." If my perm was old and I needed a touch-up, then that would make me feel insecure. I would become stressed about getting my next perm or my next fix, "I don't want them to see me like this!" A few times, I over permed my hair because I wanted to ensure it was super straight.

At first, I wasn't good at this game. I was young and trying to find my way. Most game players, other Black women who had mastered the hair game and the accepted professional look, were unwilling to share their industry secrets. So, everything that I know today is because I watched and listened to them. It wasn't an easy path for me because there were many trials and errors during my experiences; inappropriate work attire and daring hairstyles, to name a few. But I never took my eyes off the successful and professional Black women who were around me (but were not helpful toward me).

In my late twenties and early thirties, there was this emergence of the weave world. At first, I held onto the perms because I was afraid that it would not be acceptable to the other professional Black women. But as I grew older, I became braver with weaves and extensions. I realized that weave worked for me. I could be professional with it straight and black, or I could be on the cutting edge with colors, etc. I wanted to be a part of their club. I wanted to look like them and thrive in my career. Yet, I received many scars. Women would talk about me behind my back, never considering that they could help me to be like them instead. I was still determined to be a part of the winning team. I yearned to look like them and be accepted with my straight hair or weave, in their game. I was determined to get a seat at the table. This is what I had been raised and educated to do as a Black woman in the South; go to college, get a job, and learn to play the game. In addition to Black women's judgment, white women were bold enough to ask me about my choice of hairstyles on several occasions. The pressure was overwhelming, but I had to win!

By the time I was in my mid-thirties and early forties, I had lots of notes, and it seemed like I was getting closer to becoming one of them. I started wearing two-piece conservative suits (blue, black, or gray). At one point, I decided to be brave and approach one of these rule-makers, an older Black woman in an upper-level management position. I told her that I had an interest in pursuing other promotional jobs. She was more than happy to point out everything that I was doing wrong and borderline tease me for these actions. The interesting thing about this conversation is that she never gave me any advice on how to do or be better.

She was in an upper-level management position with the perfect credentials and connections. She wore nice expensive suits. Her hair was always permed and styled in a highly conservative and professional manner. I watched her. I wanted to be like her. So her rejection was a staggering blow to my esteem and self-worth! At one point, when I started dressing in the accepted conservative game uniform, she commented that she noticed I was dressing a little better.

At forty, I finally understood all of the rules. As the years continued, I would get better at "suiting" up for the game. I was more comfortable and could quickly identify and purchase work-ready clothes. I was also totally addicted and sold on the world of weave and extensions. I knew that my weave would have to look a specific way to sit at the table with the heavy hitters in the game. Yes, I had finally mastered the hair game.

As soon as I thought I was at the right place in the rat race–BAM! The natural movement began. Women are now wearing their hair in its natural state. As soon as you think you have it all figured out THEN, they change the rules. I now see more sistahs wearing kinky and curly hairdos. I also see more dreads and similar hairstyles. Then came the creation of the natural hair product lines. Social media is flooded with transition photos of sistahs leaving the perms and weaves behind to find their natural and nappy roots.

But simultaneously, I also noticed that Corporate America both public and private, are still the same. As I sit at different executive tables and engage in meetings, I've learned that the rules are still the SAME. The game makers still expect you to present as a conservative individual in professional attire. I also pay extra special attention to how a woman with natural hair is received and perceived at the executive table instead of one like me who is still playing the hair game.

The movement happened, but the rules in Corporate America never changed. So, since I had worked so damn hard to get to this place, I've decided that I want to continue to play the game. I am comfortable and confident now. I know what to wear, how to dress, and how to wear my hair. I know what to say and what to do while wearing my weave and extensions.

I also realize that those who have decided to become natural and kinky aren't always "real." Many of them shun and bully the sistahs who chose to continue to wear weaves and extensions and perm their hair. Why can't we all just get along? Why can't I wear my weave and you strut your natural or curly style, but we agree to respect each other? We don't have to look exactly alike for us to be connected as sistahs.

There is this unspoken pressure that every Black woman should now wear their hair naturally because of this recent movement. I applaud the sistahs who are rocking it like that every day. They are beautiful! But does that mean I am ugly or unworthy because I have chosen another path? The bottom line is that Black women must recognize we have become a part of the problem. We bully each other about the way we look and how we wear our hair; whether it is natural, permed, or weaved. I have worked hard to get to this point of overcoming my hair insecurities and my challenges with being accepted in the professional world. I am much wiser now, and I realize that it was never about my hair. It was about the fact that I was smart and intelligent. I'd always had everything I needed to be successful, no matter what hairstyle I chose.

2

Coiled Corporate Confusion

La Toya M. Sifford

I can remember it like it was yesterday. I was six months into graduate school, and I had just received my first job offer as a corporate trainer for one of the largest hospital systems in North Carolina. I was ecstatic; words could not express how incredible it felt to land a position in my field eight months after graduating with my bachelor's degree.

I already had "the look," I had suits for days, at least twenty-six different blazers, all colors of the rainbow, appropriate work pumps, and a genuine leather briefcase and roller bag. I was ready to show the world how polished and talented I indeed was.

On the first day on the job, all of the newly hired trainees were informed by our cohort of trainers that we would be in competition for permanent placement within the company. Everyone would not be selected to move forward with employment. I had always been an extremely competitive individual, and I knew that I would have to know the job and represent myself and the company exceptionally well for me to survive final cuts during presentations.

During that time, I was wearing my hair in a protective style, a sew-in, to be exact. Sew-ins had always been my go-to hairstyle. They came out beautiful, were easy to maintain, and they allowed me to live a life where I was not concerned about sweating out my hair at the gym. Sew-in's kept the rain from destroying my fresh blowout, hair breakage, or any other hair-raising concerns that many other Black women face today. However, with presentation day and final cuts rapidly approaching, I decided to revamp my appearance. After all, I was the youngest new hire in my cohort, and I wanted to be remembered for my skill set, professionalism, and personality after I presented. I called my hairstylist on my lunch break and booked an appointment for a silk press. I was so excited because I had been natural for two years, and this was going to be my first silk press and length check.

While on the phone with my stylist, I kept hearing voices coming from down the hallway within the building. After finalizing my appointment and saying goodbye, I hung up the phone and proceeded to follow the voices down the hall and into the break room. Upon arriving, I could see that some sort of heated discussion was taking place. I quickly scanned that room and noticed that an African American male debated how African American women should wear their natural hair in a corporate setting.

I grabbed my lunch box from the refrigerator and sat down at a table adjacent to the discussion. I had no intention of joining in because I felt this was a highly inappropriate workplace topic, just like politics and pay. Also, I was only two years into my natural hair journey. I chose to hide behind protective styles to avoid being openly bullied and harassed about my natural hair choices in public and private. The gentleman, who was most likely in his mid forties, continued on his rampage. He stated, "Natural hair is nice when tamed, but can be seen as unprofessional and tacky when not styled appropriately. Why would you just roll out of bed, take a shower, brush your teeth, and not correctly style your hair before coming into work? I just don't get it," he sighed. At the same time, a few of my co-workers chuckled at his statement. I remembered his exact words because that statement cut me deeply. I was sitting there eating my sandwich, feeling a rage build up inside of me. I thought back to when I did my big chop and how my closest family members viewed my new hairstyle.

It was around October of 2014. I had binge-watched over twenty big chop videos on YouTube and had finally built up the courage just to cut it off. I had been transitioning for a little over a year and figured what the hell, just do it; you're young, it will grow back! I can still remember all of the Google images that I had pulled up of Black women with natural hair. I had fallen in love with these images, even memorized some of them. Their hair was so coily, kinky, fuzzy, and thick. I was taken aback at how beautiful and healthy these women looked with their afros, twist, twist outs, and braid outs. So much so that I was inspired to cut my hair. Staring at myself in the mirror in my dorm room, I took the scissors and began to cut off all of my relaxed hair that had not yet fully transitioned. I stared back at myself in the mirror after cutting the last strand of dead hair, and I instantly fell in love with my mini puff. I couldn't even gather my hair into a ponytail, but I thought, so what? I was just as confident as I was when my hair was shoulder-length and relaxed, and I knew that this was my start to a healthy hair journey and a new me.

Sadly, at the time, everyone didn't share in my fondness of natural hair. Many of my family members stated their concerns regarding natural hair multiple times and showed zero support for my new hair endeavor. Like many other Black women choosing to go natural, I experienced conflict with my parents and other family members due to their expectations of how I should wear my hair and present myself to others. My parents viewed my natural hair as going backward in time, a rebellion, or some sort of internal confusion or battle that I was facing. My family felt as if straight hair was more desirable and polished and that it elevated my beauty and represented our family well. Since childhood, my mother and father have always treated me like a doll. I wore robes, heels, pageant dresses, and oversized sunglasses to grade school. I did more than tag along with my mother to her hair appointments. I received hair styling. My father even called me LaToya-Barbie. Hence, many of my family members viewed my afro and twists as inadequate representation, and attributed my rebellion to my parents lack of control over my decisions, which was far from reality. I didn't care about their opinions for a while, and I stood on the beauty that I saw in natural hair. Still, after months and months of verbal spats regarding my hair decisions and the more my family showed dislike and picked at me in private and in public about my coils, I grew less confident. I ultimately stopped styling and showcasing my natural hair altogether and reverted to sew-ins to regain their approval.

As a young adult, I never liked to rock the boat or disappoint my parents in any way, so my parent's approval meant a lot to me at the time. The last thing I wanted to do was disappoint the people who had sacrificed so much for me. I had the utmost respect for my parents, and I did not want to embarrass them or make them feel uncomfortable due to my life choices.

As I ate at the table in the break room, I continued listening to the natural hair discussion. I thought to myself; if this is how corporate-level African-Americans feel about natural hair, maybe my family members were right about my natural hair decision all along; perhaps everyone just sees me as having nappy, unmanageable hair and won't take me seriously without silky straight hair. Coming to this revelation, my stomach began to turn, and I grabbed my lunch box and quickly headed out of the break room. After work, I arrived at my hair appointment, and once in the styling chair, I asked my hairstylist to do the unthinkable. I asked my stylist to perm my hair. Yes, that's right, I asked for the creamy crack! After all, I wanted to have a fair shot in Corporate America, and I didn't want my hair to hold me back from any opportunities that I felt I deserved and had worked hard to obtain.

My hair appointment came to an end, and I looked in the large rectangular mirror hanging from the wall. My hair was limp, it had no volume, and it seemed thin and lacked luster. I instantly knew that I had made the worst decision in my entire life. That night when I arrived home, I sobbed in my bedroom for hours, so disappointed that I let the opinions of others and the stress of my appearance at work influence me into making such a terrible and hasty decision. I was heartbroken, and yet again, my family did not understand my emotions. They applauded my decision, my father, with his fresh haircut and perfectly groomed mustache, and my mother, with her auburn and blonde short, curly sew-in. They both hugged me tightly in unison, stating that they were happy to have their daughter back, but I felt far from myself.

Presentation day commenced at work, and I was chosen to move forward as a permanent corporate trainer. The panel stated that "I was very knowledgeable, energetic and presented well professionally and would be an asset to the team of corporate trainers." I was thrilled, but a part of me also felt sad. I felt like I had left behind that empowered young black woman who wanted to show Corporate America just how polished and talented she was, regardless of how her hair looked. On that day, I made another decision: the decision to transition back to being natural, and I promised myself I would not care about the opinions of others at home, at work, or anywhere else for that matter. This time I was doing it for me, and I was determined to succeed in my hair journey!

I am incredibly proud to say that I am now 100% natural at this stage in my life, and I genuinely love everything about my kinks, coils, and waves. I style my hair how I want to, and I love the attention and compliments that it brings when I am out and about. So much so that I was inspired to step out on faith and found Allure Beauty Supply, LLC in September of 2019. As Founder and CEO of Allure Beauty Supply, I feel I get to combine my new-found love of beauty products and hair care with my business experience within Corporate America.

While matriculating through my hair journey, I learned that beauty lies in a healthy mind, body, and spirit, and based on my experiences. My goal for Allure Beauty Supply is to create an educational and inspirational trendsetting hub. I want to create a place where women are greeted by someone who looks like them and offered hair care products and general hair care advice, support, and guidance regarding the styling, upkeep, and maintenance of their beautiful African-American hair, regardless of where they are in their hair journey. If I can talk someone off of the ledge and offer a compliment like I wish someone would have done for me regarding my natural hair excursion, I would consider Allure a success.

"My hair doesn't need to be fixed. Society's view of beauty is what's broken."

~ Unknown

3

Hairology 101

Cynthia Gilmore

y oldest sister, who is almost twenty-five years my senior, repeatedly says I was the cutest baby with a head full of nappy hair. Oddly, growing up, I thought my hair gave me superpowers. But despite what we thought, no one liked combing this thick, course stuff.

My living situation as a child is not what we Black folk would look at as abnormal, but others might. I lived with my maternal grandma until I was seven. I was the ninth child out of ten. My mom lived with my youngest brother's dad. My grandparents raised all their grandkids, therefore I had siblings in the same household. My brother, Rodney, was stuck with the task of doing my hair. My sister, Jennifer, had left for college and my grandma was too sick to deal with my hair. Rodney has always been very well-groomed. Most would call him a sharp dresser. I was a little nappy headed girl who was being raised mainly around boys, so I was rough and tough like them. Everyday I was scolded by Rodney for coming home from school and not looking like how I left. My hair being the source of much of his wrath, I would lose hair bows, or return home with loose ponytails, or any level of hair disarray. This hair kept me in trouble. Now don't get it twisted, I still enjoyed getting new clothes and getting all dolled up on the holidays, but I was a die-hard tomboy.

At the age of seven, I had to go live with my mom. It was during this period when I was finally introduced to the Jheri Curl, but not until after about a year of her doing my hair. A year later she and I both hated it. Now I know everyone remembers the straightening comb. This hair was so thick my mom felt she needed reinforcement. I experience so many ear burns. The tip of my right ear stayed black although I am a caramel brown beauty. I cannot remember who turned my mom on to the Jheri Curl, but I was thankful. It was around the age of nine when I was introduced to chemicals. I did not mind chemicals because they made doing my hair a little bit easier. I could deal with this nappy stuff on my own, but everyone else struggled. All I needed was a little curl activator and a pick and I could go on about my business. Everything would be cool until it was time for a touch up. Again, this nappy hair would be a little challenging because I would go six to eight weeks without really combing my hair, so when the stylist would comb it out; it was very painful. Ouch!

At the age of ten, my mom died. For a while I moved around a bit amongst my family members. The two complaints I heard upon my arrival to several of the homes I lived in were: 1.) It was a challenge to raise a girl and 2.) Her hair. I kept the Jheri Curl for a while. I wore it up until I was twelve and moved into the most stable home I would have as a child. My second mom was referred to my dad by the Department of Family and Children Services. After my mom died, I met my dad who took on the responsibility of raising me from my grandparents. He had been a truck driver since the age of nineteen and was used to living a bachelor's life. At this time, he was a long-distance driver who would be gone for weeks at a time. He needed me in a stable place, so that is how the relationship between he, and my second mom began. My second mom was probably in her mid-forties when I came into her life. It was a match made in heaven. People thought she was my biological mom. She was the woman who taught me about being a lady, knowing my worth, working hard, and playing harder. Mom had a cousin who had her own hair salon and started taking me to her on a regular basis. When I began middle school, I asked could I get rid of the Jheri Curl and get a perm. Mom got permission from my dad and I transitioned to the straight side. My stylist/cousin always talked about how thick my hair was. I remember her and the other stylist laughing at me because my hair would just absorb the perm. I suffered from a lot of chemical burns because my stylist always used super strength and it seemed like it would take forever for my hair to get straight. Not knowing any better, I thought the pain of the process was normal. I did not complain because I loved the end results. A monster was created because for years after getting that first perm, I lived in hair salons.

My dad was a dark-skinned man from Dothan, AL. That is where he was raised until he moved to Tampa, FL as a teenager. It was no secret that Dad loved fair-skinned or white women as love interests. Number two, my second mom and he never dated because he considered her to be "too dark" for him. Mind you, she was a shade darker than me. During my transition of going from a Jheri Curl to a perm, I had to get my hair cut due to the damage caused from me not combing it properly. I loved the short look and did not have any problems rocking it. But my dad...my dad on the other hand had a fit to the point where he cursed my second mom out and whipped me, stating "Do not cut your hair anymore." I thought to myself, "What is the big deal. It's just hair; it will grow back." My dad felt if he was paying for my hair I could not cut it. It was around this time when I started noticing how men would compare women, and that there was a preference for those who had lighter- skin and long flowing hair.

At the age of fourteen I started working so I could pay for my own hair appointments. I have always been strong willed and I've always done as I pleased. I stopped going to my cousin and found myself a young male stylist who worked at the South Dekalb Mall. Tremone and I were a great pair because he was working on setting himself apart from the other local stylists and I was young, bold, and daring. I felt about my hair the way most people feel about shoes; as long as my hair was laid, I had on some earrings, and little gloss, I was good. I would go from short to long, tried all kinds of colors, and stayed getting compliments. People would also notice right away when my hair was not done. My guy friends would be quick to say "what's wrong with your hair" when it was not done. I learned that by keeping this nappy hair done, I gained a lot of attention. I did not grow up disliking light-skinned, long haired girls or girls who had "good hair" no matter their skin color because my hair stayed on point.

As I started getting older, going through life's journeys, I realized when I was going through a trying time, it was reflected through my hair styles. As I said, as a teenager I lived in the hair salons. I have worn almost any style you could think of and sometimes would get my hair done twice a week. I feel this reflected the turmoil I lived as a teenager. I lost my mom at an early age and was left with my male chauvinist, misogynistic, color struck dad for whom I never felt I was good enough for. I experienced being raped and molested. I never felt loved or appreciated as a child and both were things I longed for. I became a single mom at eighteen and now have four wonderful children. At times, life would get extremely hard and I would have to go through periods of not getting my hair done and I would have to deal with this nappy hair myself. I would feel embarrassed and ashamed because I could not have my superb hair do's. In my mid-thirties, I discovered I suffered from depression and anxiety. I worked hard and sacrificed a lot trying to raise my kids. I sacrificed so much that at times I just let myself go and stopped doing the things that I enjoyed such as getting my hair done.

October of 2020 made two years that I have been on my natural hair journey. I felt I was beginning to make some positive transitions in my life as I continued to follow the lead of my now sixteen-year-old daughter. You see, at the age of ten, my daughter announced she no longer wanted chemicals in her hair and had her grandma do the "big chop." I was so mad at them and told her, "I don't know who was going to do all that thick hair!" One of my sista friends scolded me for not being supportive of my baby girl. She said I should be proud that she was secure in herself and confident enough to embrace her natural beauty. Once I thought about it, I knew she was right and gained admiration for my daughter because this situation reminded me of the times when I was bold and fearless as well.

My daughter taught herself how to care for her hair via YouTube and now has a beautiful mane of natural hair. After watching her over the last six years, I got the courage to go through with my own big chop. The first year I was extremely uncomfortable. I had been dealing with breakage and was very self-conscious of the spot in my hair where the breakage had occurred. I would ask my daughter if I were still cute? Did I look gay? There were also a few times when I was contemplating going back to chemicals. Then once I realized the convenience of having natural hair: it takes less time and it's less expensive and I enjoy the ability to just get up and go. So, that first year I allowed my hair to grow and I colored it, while trying to figure it all out. Then I went through a second big chop, which I am loving.

I rock a little afro that I colored honey-blonde. I get compliments daily, but I do not think it is just about my hair. In addition to loving what's on the outside, I have also found more peace and self-love within myself. I find myself smiling more and interacting with people differently. I am not as brass as I used to be and I am not always on the defense.

I have conquered many trials and tribulations throughout my lifetime and I consider myself a warrior princess. I now understand that it's not about my hair, weight, the car I drive, or other material things I possess, but instead it is about my character, values, views, self-love, and preservation. My hair compliments the sweet and loving spirit that shines from within me. My hair does not define me, instead, I define my hair.

4

Choices & Mind Shifts

Hanaiya Payne-Johnson

*G*rowing up as a young girl in South Northeast Texas to be exact, I remember being taught, "A woman is only as beautiful as her hair." It was never verbally spoken, but rather shown through the actions of others. For generations, the women in my family took pride in growing their hair as long as it would possibly grow. Haircuts consisted of the clipping of ends on the new moon, which is another story for another day. I took it as an honor to be a part of a heritage of women with long flowing hair. Saturdays were dedicated to press and curls in preparation for Sunday worship. What I did not see was women wearing their hair in its natural state. I did not see women with wash and go's or locs. I only saw straight hair around me, with some wearing relaxers while others opted for blow outs, but the results were always the same...straight hair. I often wondered why

I could not just wash my hair and let it flow in the wind as God had created it to do.

Being the youngest of four girls, my mothers' pride was to see her daughters with perfectly maintained hair. We could never leave the house looking any kind of way as long as we were under her roof. Our hair had to be done to perfection. She did not allow us to get relaxers but chillleee we endured the hot comb, grease and gas stove for perfectly straight hair and for special occasions we had the privilege of Shirley temple curls that were then rolled with a brown paper sack or those horrible pink sponge rollers. But again, I questioned why I was having to alter my hair? Why could I not wear my hair in it's natural, thick wooly state once it was washed and air dried. In the back of my mind I thought, "I am going through all of this to sweat and have grease running all down my neck and face?" We lived in Texas and there is nothing worse than the smell of a fresh sweaty press and curl. Imagine the smell of hot burning licorice and you have exactly what I felt I smelled like.

I remember being about six years old and promising myself that when I got older, I was never straightening my hair again, however it grew was how I was going to wear it. I'd had enough of that darn stove and hot comb, while holding my ear to make sure the tip of it did not get burned. I was tired of using an entire day just to do my hair. But I always heard the echo, "You need to look decent and with your hair all over your head you will not go far in life." So, I would just roll my eyes and shake the thought of wearing my hair natural, away.

Once as a teen I decided to not straighten my hair and just wear it as we like to say "natural" because I still was not yet getting relaxers. The excitement to just wash, comb it out and put a little mousse and go had me feeling like I was floating on a cloud. Relishing in the fact that I would not have to take fifteen minutes to wrap my hair that night to perfection then tie two scarves around to keep my hair nice and smooth was like being on the vacation of a lifetime. However, that vacation was short lived. I forgot I was growing up in a small town in Texas where everyone was used to the same ole daily routines. The looks I received and the "Oh my can I touch it," made me go right back to straightening my hair. I was over it. I remember plastering a fake smile saying please do not touch my hair as my palms would become sweaty from just the idea of someone invading my personal space. It was upsetting. The audacity of these people asking such ridiculous questions. It was not just Caucasians, but people that looked just like me asking to touch or feel my hair. It outraged me. It was like saying "Hey, can I have a bite of your hamburger?" HECK NO!!!

I was over it to the point that as a seventeen year old senior in high school, I had my oldest sister take me for what she thought was a trim but ended up being me cutting my hair which was four inches from my waist to right below my ears. The look on her face was priceless, her chin was literally laying on her chest when she realized I was chopping my hair off. I, on the other hand, was smiling bigger than a kid in a Kool-Aid commercial. It was as if a huge weight had been lifted off my shoulders. I still continued to straighten my hair through college and not let it grow past my shoulders because I was a little traumatized from the first wash and go experience.

When I became an adult, I continued to straighten my hair because it was just a part of who I thought I was. I was straightening my hair to make my day go a little smoother without people staring or walking up touching my hair or asking the infamous question, "Where did you buy that hair?" I could handle the question, "Is that your real hair" or asking what type of hair I had purchased, better than the people touching my head. When people would ask me where I bought my hair, I would always answer sarcastically, "D & W" with a smirk on my face as I walked off. Laughing now, I know those poor women went on an endless hunt in search of D & W Hair Supply on Google, a store none of them would ever find because those are the first name initials of my parents.

One day my need to straighten my hair, changed. I remember like it was yesterday, I was at work and my Boss, an older Asian woman, said to me, "I am so glad you are different from them." Now at that moment, my blood began to boil, my pulse quickened and my forehead became sweaty. I told myself to stay calm and not to let her get me out of character, but my face began to share my feelings. I know it was saying "I know like hell you did not just say that to me?!" I have a habit of tilting my head to the side and narrowing my eyes, while clenching my lips together, when I am frustrated. I remember looking to the left to gather my thoughts, which I absolutely had to do in that moment before asking exactly who she was referring to when she said "them." As an older Asian woman in her mid-fifties, I felt she should have known better than to make such a statement. She should have known what it felt like to be discriminated against for being a minority and a woman. She, as I expected, said "You know these new young Blacks that just wear their hair all over their head and look like they have never seen a comb. I realized that she, like so many others, judged women with melanated skin, by something as simple as a personal choice of hairstyle, and in her opinion, curls and coils equaled inadequate. The crazy thing is I expected that from a middle-aged Caucasian male, but not her.

My subconscious took me back to that six-year-old little girl in Northeast Texas who often asked the question, "Why am I straightening my hair?" Do we as women of color straighten our hair because it makes us think we look good, or have we been trained to do it because it makes Mainstream America feel more comfortable? Do we think we look less urban? I was confused as to how this woman, who only knew me in a work setting and only knew me as an employee, thought she had me all figured out based on my hair. Instead of threatening her with going to HR, I decided to handle it my way and show her that I was the "them" she was so afraid of.

I was no longer concerned about anyone being comfortable around me based on my hair. See it is just that my hair and I am free to do as I please. Whether I choose to wash and go, or take all day to straighten it, it's my choice. That day I decided to go back to that promise I made as a six year old little girl. At the age of twenty-four I stopped straightening my hair with relaxers and just let it be free. I decided that the act of straightening my hair would only be done if it was something I wanted to do, not because I felt I had to conform to society and its standards.

I made sure to start telling my three-year-old daughter at the time, how beautiful her natural wooly curls were and to be proud to wear them however she chooses and to never allow another person to push their hair views on her. I never wanted her to have that same question of, "Why am I straightening my hair," but not ever knowing the answer. Black women being able to be versatile with our hair has always been a rite of passage from the Afro to the Jheri Curl, we can rock it all with no problem.

After about three months, my hair began to get bulky and nappy, as Blacks say. But what was really taking place was my thick hair was finally returning back to its natural glory. With pride, I washed my hair and just let it do its thang. The next day I walked into my job in Corporate America with the biggest smile, then I walked right into my boss's office. She looked mortified. If only I had a camera to capture her expression. I felt calm as a cucumber. My boss, on the other hand, was frantic. She began to stutter and get all nervous, saying " Oh my, what is going on? Are you ok?" I responded, "I feel perfectly fine," as I fingered my curls. "How are you?" I asked. She responded with, "Did you forget we have a client meeting today? Just run home and straighten your hair or pull it into a ponytail." To which I replied, "Oh my hair? As in my natural hair? You do not think it is appropriate?" I almost sang the words in order to keep from laughing in her face. Whether I am wearing my hair curly or straight, my knowledge does not change. She finally responded and indicated that it was just more professional to wear it straight. See for her it was more professional because her hair grows straight, mine does not. It grows in waves and patterns that frame my face, highlight my high cheekbones and the large nose that God gave this Black queen. I responded as calmly as I knew how, "I am sorry if my appearance offends you, but it is who I am and I am no longer changing me to make the likes of you comfortable," I smiled and proceeded to go prepare for my presentation. To say she was upset is an understatement. She was red as a cherry tomato in the face and would have spit fire if she could.

The glory and satisfaction I felt to stand up for me and my crown was truly a stepping stone for my confidence. We went into our meeting and not one word was said by our client about my hair, now they may have been shocked because they were not used to seeing it in that state, but my hair did not take away anything from the presentation. In fact, I feel the newfound confidence enhanced my performance that day.

From that day forward, I decided if I went on a job interview and comments were made about my hair or I could tell it made them uncomfortable, I would know that was not the place for me. My hair has absolutely nothing to do with my skill set or who I am as a person. Do I straighten my hair at times, sure I do, it is just part of being a woman. We all express ourselves at times through our hair style choices. The fact of the matter remains, whether I am rocking braids, a wash and go or a bone straight style, it is my personal right and choice.

Society has dictated who and what we as women of color should look like, feel, and how we should react. I am grateful that we no longer allow the world to dictate how we wear our hair. It saddens me and excites me that we now have the Crown Act to protect our right to show self-expression through our hair. Should an actual bill have had to be passed by The United States Congress to protect people from being discriminated against because of something as simple as their hair, absolutely not. It should have just been a natural right like breathing. We have no control over the hair color or texture we are born with.

The Crown Act and conversation we are starting to have regarding hair discrimination are well overdue. Black women and men have been degraded and penalized for far too long for existing simply as he or she was born, Starting with slavery, we were made to cover it, or cut it off and then denied access to care for our own hair. Hair in the Black community has always been and will always be a tool of self-expression. We can look back to our ancestors and look at the elaborate hairstyles worn or even the great Afro movement of the seventies. It gives my heart joy that now my fourteen-year-old daughter will be able to go into the workplace and wear her hair as she chooses without the fear of discrimination for being herself. I pray that one day all states will pass the Crown Act and realize that the original seven states were right on target with making America great.

5

Hair Affair

Deckquelynn E. Burks

At a time when most young girls are deciding what the future holds after high school, I was faced with bigger challenges. You see, there I was, a fresh eighteen-year old, with nothing on her mind but completing high school and attending the best historically Black college and university (HBCU) on the planet, Southern University A&M College in Baton Rouge, Louisiana. It was early May, three weeks until my high school graduation, when a trip to the doctor had gone terribly wrong. Seven months prior, I had complained to my mother and then pediatrician about an unexplainable pain in the crest of my left hip. Routine tests were done, and the prognosis was always the same. My doctors would chime "You're still extremely young to be hearing this, but dear, this is an unusual case of arthritis." I took the prescribed medication. My pain was of course only temporarily numbed and then it began to intensify with a vengeance. There were more tests, more blood work, and finally, an x-ray. The second most traumatic thing anyone has ever said to me was about to be spoken, and as anyone might imagine, I was not ready to receive the verdict.

"How have you been feeling?" My doctor asked.

"If I'm being honest, I have been tremendously drained. I am having a hard time sleeping, and the pain is either waking me up in the middle of the night or won't subside, even after taking the prescribed medication. What is happening?" I responded. "My dear, I need to speak with you about some of the tests you had done last week." "Oh. Okay." By this time, I am certain, my heartbeat could be heard coming down the hallway of my doctor's office. "I am so sorry to have to tell you this, but…you have cancer. It is a very aggressive form but can be treated if it is caught in enough time."

"What is enough time?"

"The type we have determined that you have is called Hodgkin's Lymphoma or Hodgkin's Disease. There are four stages to Hodgkin's and my dear, you are in the last stage, Stage IV-B." My doctor said very remotely.

"So, what's after Stage IV-B?" I nervously asked.

"Death. I know you will need some time to process what is going on with you, but because of the shift of this disease, we need to move quickly. I am recommending chemotherapy immediately following a bone biopsy which will be one week from today." It was a Friday Afternoon. "Are there any other immediate questions you have about the procedure you're having next week?"

"Just one."

"I'm all ears."

"You mentioned chemotherapy right?"

"That is correct."

"Will…will I lose my hair doctor?"

"Yes, yes I'm afraid that you will."

I did not speak for the duration of that visit. For anyone who has ever known me will tell you, the one thing I never played about up to that point in my life was my hair. I was taught to embrace my then very thick, semi-wavy, half-way down my back, coarse black hair. I have horrid stories of the hot comb from hell like many girls growing up in the seventies and eighties, but to talk against my hair was a slap in the face. How would I breathe without it I wondered? As my mother communicated the traumatic news to immediate family, I became more and more numb and quite aloof about what I was about to face and be up against. My worry however was not initially about beating cancer or the chemotherapy itself, it was me losing my hair. How on earth would I recover from that? It was June 1992.

By November 1993, I had undergone two types of chemotherapy, that my body rejected, and had five surgeries. My health and immune system were rapidly declining. My last and only option was to have extremely high doses of chemo, followed by a bone marrow transplant using my own marrow. In 1993, this type of thing was unheard of. I would become part of a test study of patients who would have their bone marrow taken out of their bodies, cleaned, and slowly filtered back into the body. This was the beginning of Stem Cell Research. I was making history and did not know it. What wasremarkable also, was that after twelve weeks of chemo, I had not lost one strand of hair. My emotions were plastered everywhere about awaiting my hair loss at that point. Hair loss to me was associated with unattractiveness, unsexy, uncool, unpopular, and unappealing (at least that was my eighteen-year-old perspective). Each week, I would cringe and dash to the mirror to see if there was any shedding, any breakage, or anything abnormal happening to my hair. There wasn't. I agreed to the high dosage of chemo followed by the bone marrow transplant using my own bone marrow, but I was clear on one thing to my mother and to my family, this for me would be my end of the road. I was so fatigued and drained. My then nineteen-year-old body had already had enough. I thought I had run a good race. I had fought the fight. I was done. On the second round of high dose chemo, it happened. Completely caught me off guard. My hair was coming out, and not just a few strands, but by the hand full. My mom was leaving for the day to go home and get some much-needed rest as my aunt Wendy was coming to spend the night with me in the hospital. I asked my mom to brush my hair back because the low-grade fever I was having had somehow made me even hotter. As she brushed, she gasped.

"Mama what's wrong? Why do you keep doing that?" I groggily asked her.

"Your hair."

"What about it?"

"It's...coming out. It has finally decided to...come out."

"Brush it all out!" I replied, as the waterworks began to sting my eyes. The moment I was dreading since the beginning of this whole ordeal had arrived without any warning. That for me meant I would have to now focus on the cancer and the now five of eight people who remained alive in the bone marrow unit. I didn't want that to be my reality.

"I don't think..."

"Mama, please! This is already hard enough. Brush...it all out." She obliged.

Let me first say that shopping for a wig was not for me. I didn't understand the patience nor did I have the knowledge to spend a perfectly good day in a wig shop Looking for textures, colors and styles of make-believe hair. My hair was a very real thing, and far more than dear to me. Wearing a wig felt like some type of betrayal to my hair that I no longer had. I mean, it had been with me for all my then nineteen years, yet being without it brought on a new insecurity I had never known. Eventually, I agreed with my aunt Wendy and mother who encouraged me to go wig shopping before I began high dosage chemotherapy rounds. After what felt like forty-eight hours instead of the two hours I was in the shop, I was prepared for when the devastating day would arrive. I began wearing one of two human hair wigs that replicated pretty-closely the style, color and length of my own natural hair. My medical staff were none the wiser until two days into my actual bone marrow transplantation. One night, I encountered a high fever and had to shed an article of something, I threw my wig across the room. What I found hilarious was that neither my doctor nor his nursing staff knew that I had transitioned into a wig because of the length of time it took me to lose my hair compared to…well, almost everyone else who had the same diagnosis. My family and I would joke about perhaps it was a black thing. Wouldn't be the first-time a woman of color made a groundbreaking discovery about hair.

Three days into having my marrow filtered back into my frail body, grave news came. My liver was shutting down, my fever was rising even higher and my body was rejecting the process. Time for me stood still. I recall hearing mumbling in the hallway as my doctor spoke to my mother, and words like clergy and funeral home were spoken. I will never forget the look on my mother's sunken face when she re-entered my room.

"I don't want you to be alarmed or upset, but I just requested for our Pastor to come and have a few words with you."

Groggily, I asked, "Mama, what's going on?"

"Just try and rest. He will be here shortly."

On my tray table was my Bible, a purple ink pen, a small pitcher of ice water, the television remote and a box of half eaten Chicken McNuggets my younger brother Ty had gotten for me from the downstairs McDonald's. I opened my bible, read a few chapters in Psalms and dozed off. I guess a few hours had passed when I awoke to a very distinctive and familiar voice. It was my Pastor.

"How have you been feeling?" He asked initially.

"Fine on some days… tired and sick on other days."

"Such a time as this, it is a blessing to be surrounded with your loved ones. I see your mother, brother, grandmother, aunts and uncles are all here with you."

"They are?"

"Yes, they are right across the hall in the waiting room." It was Thanksgiving weekend.

"Oh." I didn't know what else to add to that.

"I have a very important question to ask you. I see you have a bible here on your table. Have you talked to God? Have you prayed to be healed? Are you praying?" "Do I pray Pastor? That's all I do." I answered, trying to sit up but realized I was much too weak to do so.

From my understanding, I again drifted off to sleep. What happened next still has me at a loss for words when I think about it. I had a near death experience. I know there are people who do not believe this happens or occurs, but I'm here to tell you just how real and remarkable it was. At first it felt like a foggy dream. My maternal great-grandfather appeared (who passed when I was in the first grade). I of course remembered and immediately recognized him. What was most compelling was what was behind him. It was a hint of light. As he spoke to me and talked, I began walking forward. Looking around his six plus feet of stature to gain a better look at that light. I asked if he could take me to his house. He stated he could not. I didn't hear much of anything else from him. The light grew bigger, more distinct and now calming even. Next appeared a paternal great-aunt who died the year before I was born. She too asked how I was feeling and called me beautiful. I recalled asking her if I could go to her house. She told me no. She talked and said a few more things as I continued to walk forward. She was walking backward. The light was so very bright that it felt like a full moon surrounded by a million stars, but the stars felt within reach. I felt I should have had on shades. My eyes did not hurt, but they were widened. I began looking around her petite frame and long silver hair to gain a better view of this light that had captured my attention. She eventually dissolved and then appeared my maternal great-grandmother who died when I was in the seventh grade. Immediately recognizing her, I looked away for a milli-second. She inquired about how things were going. I was honest in telling her that things were not going well. Now, my Big-Mama was not only considered a wise woman, but she was a very healthy and stock solid woman, so trying to maneuver around her to once again see what my fascination was with this light was becoming a bit more difficult. As she inched slightly forward, I found myself taking tiny steps backwards. I thought me asking her to take me to her house would also cause her to dissolve, but not my Big-Mama.

"Big-Mama, can I come home with you?"

"You don't want to really come to my house, do you?"

She was throwing me off my game. In this space with her, I had not once worried or cared about anything. I was not aching, hurting, tired, anxious, restless, and most importantly, bald. I was smart not to respond, because somehow, I felt she already knew I could care less about going to her house unless it would bring me closer to the array of lights that were twinkling and blinking behind her.

"What is that behind you? What is that light?"

"I'm not here to talk to you about what that is behind me. I am here to tell you that if you want to go home with me, you won't see your mama and your family no mo', and you don't want to do that do you?"

Again, I felt my inner Diva betraying me.

"I think they will be okay if I don't see them anymore. Yeah, they might be sad, but they'll be okay. So, does that mean I can go to your house now?" I asked, with probably too much enthusiasm.

"If you go to my house with me...you won't be able to go to Southern." My Big-Mama said matter-of-factly. "Southern? Big-Mama, you know about Southern?" I was beyond amazed, and now still in my tracks. The lights were becoming more and more distinct and distant. Everything was back to pitch black. From the moment I was in the seventh grade, if not before, all I could think about was going to Southern University in Baton Rouge, Louisiana. Maybe it had to do with the then new tv show called '*A Different World*' which chronicled the life of students attending an HBCU. Maybe it was because my aunts Carol and Stephanie were in college when I was in the seventh grade, and I would soak up nearly everything either had to say about what they or their friends were doing in college. Or, perhaps it was my Aunt Deloris who had graduated from Southern when I was only two, but she made it sound like a cloud of decadent chocolate that you could devour every day, and I love me some chocolate. There was no way my dead great-grandmother was to know the slightest thing about me wanting to go to Southern at all, or so my nineteen-year-old-self thought. "Yeah, I know about Southern!" She chuckled. "I know about a lot."

I didn't want to think about what all she could have meant by that, but I awoke as I would from a night of regular sleep. What I did not know was that I had been in a light coma-like state for almost three weeks. As much as I wanted to leave my illness and everything that had been attached to it, I returned to that room, that bed, that pain, the baldness and the awful medications all in hopes to potentially one day attend and graduate from Southern University. Me returning to my hospital bed meant I had to fight and give it my all if I had any shot to once and for all beat cancer and get my hair back. What was most devastating, yet remarkable, was that of the eight people who entered the bone marrow unit, I was the only survivor. For those in the back who maybe did notread that, I WAS THE ONLY SURVIVOR! I would progress on to radiation every day for five months and by May 1994, I was cleared with full remission and a new head and texture of hair. I was finally able to fulfill my dream of attending and graduating from Southern. My first two courses (which were taken that same summer) were Introduction to Psychology (my major) and advanced Freshman English.

My hair, if you're wondering, is back healthy (not quite as thick) but is past shoulder length and is just as much my crowning glory. What I discovered during my journey of illness was truly how short, yet precious life really is. With so much unnecessary drama and negativity that plagues the world today, shouldn't the discussion of one's hair be irrelevant? Whether you are a sista who prefers to rock her natural curls and coils, relaxed (permed), wet and wavy, afro or weaves and wigs, do your thing sis. The only true approval you should need to be worried about is your own, and please know, God is merciful and able! This is my testimony.

6

Lack of Hair Esteem

Nyrobi Wheeler, MBA, CPRW

Throughout my years on this earth, I have had good and bad days with my hair being either too frizzy or too dry or realizing my scalp is sensitive to certain products. I love my hair to a certain extent. I love the fact that I was blessed with naturally curly hair, but I wish I could have grown it at least to my shoulders, being able to silk press it and make it beautiful. I have tried to extend the length of my hair by adding extensions or weave as they call it or wearing wigs, but these methods only cause my natural hair to break off. Overall, I guess you can say I sometimes suffered from what I call a "lack of hair esteem." I love the way Octavia Spencer said it in the Netflix movie, *Self-Made: Inspired by the Life of Madame CJ Walker*, "I had a Cain versus Abel relationship with my hair."

Growing up in a mid-sized Midwestern town, I was pretty much a happy only child. I loved school and enjoyed playing with train sets versus dolls. Looking back at some pictures of me as a child, I always wondered why my hair looked different in some pictures versus others – some having a big curly afro versus almost bald. I was curious about what happened to my hair, and when I inquired, I was told that my hair fell out when I was around the age of six years old due to eczema, which I subconsciously do not remember. I was told that my eczema was hereditary. Eczema or Atopic Dermatitis is a skin condition that causes the skin to be inflamed or irritated due to allergies caused by certain foods or outdoor pollution. Eczema can start in early childhood and is common among African Americans. In my case, I would have flare ups when my skin was dry. These occurred when the weather was hot and humid. My parents did the best they could to treat my symptoms by keeping my skin moist, giving me vitamins, and making sure I ate healthy foods.

Throughout my life, I've endured various emotional experiences that steam from my hair. As an adolescent, I wore a short Jheri Curl style, but I was made fun of in both middle and high school because of it. In high school, I changed my hairstyle and went from having a short Jheri Curl to putting a relaxer in my hair and using a curling iron to make it stand out. It was my hope that this style would boost my self-esteem.

As an adult, unfortunately, the emotional traumas have continued, with the bullies now being adults. In adulthood, I've experienced my fair share of discrimination regarding my hair both in the workplace and in public settings. Within the workplace, some of my colleagues have made statements about my hair, saying that it looks good in short curly styles, while others have made hurtful comments, stating that my short styles made my face look fatter. While working in a university setting, where the office was predominantly white, my past co-workers were surprised when I decided to rock a light red hair color. The disgust on their faces showed whenever they saw me. I just ignored them because I was a hard worker and I should not have been judged based on my appearance if it did not interfere with my work responsibilities.

I have also experienced hair discrimination in personal settings. While traveling on public transportation, I have had strangers make nasty comments about my hair such as my hair is too frizzy or my short fade cut makes me look like a guy, even when I am wearing makeup and earrings. At one point there was an older white lady who lived in my apartment complex that made nasty comments not just about my hair, but about me in general. She would make statements such as, "She keeps her hair short because she is too lazy to comb it, or why are you wearing your hair like that because it makes you look fat." There were days when she would make these comments and I would just cry when I got home.

There are many issues that can have a major effect on self-esteem, including your hair. In my case, I cannot change my hair texture, which was impacted by eczema, but what I did discover is that I can change my hairstyles and color as often as I like, which helps to boost my self-esteem and self-confidence. Within the last few years my hairline has started greying. Now I could take this as another blow to my self-confidence, but I don't. Instead, I use coloring to cover up those grey hairs (my favorite hair color at the moment is honey blonde). I am learning how to embrace the uniqueness of my hair and to stop caring what people think of it. I am still evolving, and slowly beginning to understand that as long as I feel good about myself and about my hair, that's all that matters.

7

Being Naturally Me is Enough

Rashauna C. Arnold, MA, CPRW, CPCC

THE EARLY YEARS – NO HAIR AND I DO CARE

Lord, where do I begin with my hair journey? Let's start with my first toddler photo, of a cute little brown baby, propped up on a white and fluffy pillow. The only distinction of me being a little girl was a red bow barrette placed in the center of my head. I honestly don't know how my mom pulled that off because I didn't have enough hair to put into a respectable ponytail or braids. But I give my mother her props for trying. My mother "tried" for several years to keep the little amount of hair laid and maintained on my head. But it was not enough to prevent the onslaught of teasing on the playground. "You bald-headed!" All the Black boys and girls would say, then followed by laughs and finger-pointing. "Your hair is so little." All the non-black kids would say, almost in amazement as to how that would be possible. Everybody in the school and even the janitor referred to me as "bald-headed". It really couldn't get any lower than that for me. All I ever wanted was for my hair to touch my shoulders. Then, everyone would leave me alone. Then, I would feel "pretty." At seven years old, I had already been reminded over and over that something was wrong with me because of my hair. I would do all I could to fill that void of insecurity by standing in the mirror combing and pulling down my hair in hopes it would help it grow. I would wear pretty scarves to make buns and ponytails out of them while walking around the house so I could at least feel something draping from my head. It was pretty sad.

MY FIRST RELAXER – AND THE YEARS OF BURNING, ITCHING SCALP, AND DRYNESS

By the age of seven, my mother gave in to the creamy crack and gave me my first kid relaxer. She did what any hard-working mother would do to help ease her stress with my 4C hair at the time in the ninety's. I honestly try not to remember this experience because it was rather traumatizing. My mom would place me in the tub, part my hair, and slap a bunch of thick white cream on my head. Then she'd dump huge cups of water on top of my head while yelling, "Don't open your eyes!" Being the hard-headed kid I was, I peeked just a little bit and my eyes burned like hell! It wasn't a good day for me. Actually, things weren't good for several years after that day. My scalp became inflamed with huge, dry, and flaky clumps of dandruff. Every week, my mom would have me sit on the floor between her legs to comb out the flakes in my hair before anyone could see me the week ahead. It was terrible! She tried covering the flakes by spraying oil sheen on my scalp, but that really didn't do too much. The relaxers did not help my hair growth at all. Nor did the ritual of slapping on globs of hair grease and straightening my hair with a hot comb over the stove as the hot grease popped on my "kitchen." By this time, I was ready to go bald and throw on a wig, and I wasn't even 10 years old yet!

THE RELAXER THAT STOLE MY EDGES

By age fourteen, my mother had been giving me relaxers pretty regularly. So, I had become accustomed to our hair routine, the excess grease, and the flaky scalp. My hair never did grow to my shoulders as I had wanted, and the bullying didn't stop either. But to be honest, my hair actually didn't look so bad. It was well kept in a cute little wrap. But no one wants a cute little wrap as a kid. We all wanted long hair and ponytails with colorful hair clips. And if you didn't have long hair, someone at any given time would remind you that you were indeed "bald-headed."

I remember when I started doing my own relaxers. I thought I was grown I guess and moved up from the kiddie relaxers to the adult relaxers. I made this move perhaps a bit too soon. I bypassed a regular adult relaxer and went straight to a super relaxer. If I came across one on a shelf right now, I'd buy it just to run over it! The day I used this relaxer for the first time, I did my normal routine of rinsing it out in the shower. As I ran my fingers through my scalp, I noticed clumps of hair sticking to them. I thought perhaps I was just trippin' and didn't just feel a chunk of hair wisp through my fingers and onto the shower floor. But I kept my eyes closed and kept rinsing because the burning was increasing, and it had to come out. I opened my eyes slowly, hoping the cool breeze I felt on the back of my head was just a cool wind creeping in from the bathroom window on that early spring day. It wasn't. My hair had indeed fallen out! Chunks of hair were on the floor, I was so shocked by what I saw that I didn't even scream. I couldn't even cry. I just went completely numb. I nearly tripped over the tub scurrying out to look into the mirror to see about a good two inches of edges wiped away from around my entire head. I lifted my hair up to see only patches of faded hair and scalp. The look could've been a style worn proudly if it were ten or so odd years later, you know, the one where women taper their sides and back but keep their hair long on the top. But this wasn't that time. It was literally the turn of the twenty-first century and I was fourteen. I didn't know what I was doing with my hair. My mother was just as shocked as I was. She tried to make me feel good by telling me that my hair was long enough to cover up the escaped edges and that the hair would grow back. So, I went to school as usual and for about a month, my mother would moisturize what was left of my edges and we prayed for them to grow back... quickly.

One day in class my so-called friend felt the need to let me know that she could see through my hair and noticed I had no edges. I was embarrassed. When school was over, I rushed home to plead with my mom about finding help to remedy the situation because walking home that day, the wind had my hair flying upward, with my bald edges exposed. I was beyond annoyed. It was the fall semester and I was in the eighth grade. There was no way I was going to make it to graduation with this mess on my head. My mother made a few quick calls to family and friends. I had seven aunties and several female cousins, and my mom had lots of girlfriends. Someone was bound to help me. I was soon referred to a hair salon where the owner was apparently known for growing hair. Let's just say his name was Tom. Tom booked us an appointment two weeks after my epic meltdown. It felt like the longest two weeks of my life.

THE HAIR SALON AND A BIG CHOP

Finally, my appointment with Tom was here! Off I went to the hair salon. I was so ecstatic. I'd heard great things about Tom and knew that whatever he would offer was better than what my mother and I had attempted with my head. We took the Red Line 'L' train from the North Side to the South Side of Chicago. It was almost a two-hour trip. My mother and I finally arrived at the hair salon, but Tom wasn't ready for me, so I had to wait.

I didn't mind waiting because I knew he would figure out what was wrong, give me something to help my edges grow back, and voilà! I'd finally have some long healthy hair.

Well, the complete opposite happened. He looked at my head and explained that the damage from the relaxer is what caused my hair to fall out and trying to maintain it by using special products would not help it grow back fast. The best option would be to chop it off! OMG, the worst thing that could possibly happen, is happening. He could see on my face that I was devastated by his answer and reassured me that he would make it look cute and it would take my hair about six months to grow back. He even had me talk to a lady in his shop who also chopped her hair off due to relaxer damage and she now had hair down her back. I wasn't trying to hear any of that because six months to a fourteen year old is eternity. He swiveled my chair to face the mirror and started to go to work. I refused to look at the mirror and instead opted to gaze at the floor in distress as the scissors clipped chunks of my hair off. He gave me a relaxer still, which I thought was rather strange. But nonetheless, hours later, he finished. I looked in the mirror and saw his version of the "Halle Berry" hairdo. I looked like an old lady. My hair was nice, but this was just not the hairstyle for a fourteen year old who wanted to look her age, I looked like an old lady. Some of the ladies in the salon tried complimenting me, but it came off as more patronizing than anything. I figured if I dropped dead right now, it would save me the misery I would endure the week ahead at school.

I didn't want to go to school that week. That Monday I waited right until five minutes before the bell rang before I walked across the street for the first period to start. I walked in and noticed some people staring, shocked faces, and questions asking why I cut my hair. But no one ridiculed me as much as I'd thought they would. It was more of an awkward, "don't say anything" kind of energy. God was definitely looking down and giving me the grace I needed because I definitely couldn't bear any more ridicule.

Every other week, my mom and I would travel across the city to the salon to get my hair done. I didn't care for the hair salon. I thought it was utterly ridiculous and unprofessional to have clients sit in a salon for hours on end. The average wait time was eight hours. His business really wasn't that busy to me, but when you add the time for smoke breaks, candy breaks, disputes with customers in and outside of the salon, I had plenty of time to get all of my homework done. The good thing about the salon was that it was a few blocks from my grandmother's house. I always felt safe and comfortable being around her. She showered me with compliments of being smart, classy, and pretty. I never felt bad about my hair length. And although most of my female cousins had long hair down their backs and were mistaken at times for having "Indian" in them, I was never made to feel bad about my lack of hair. So at least I had that reprieve from the peers at school and was grateful for that.

The sixth month passed, and my hair was not down my back, but it was healthy and growing. Now my new hair ritual of going to the salon every two weeks was kept through high school. I'd still get teased from time to time. At every six-week trim, Tom would cut my ends a little shorter. I didn't really think too much of it at first, but over time it seemed like he kept cutting my hair once I'd reached my hair goals.

HAIR COLOR AND THE EPIC BETRAYAL

Junior year of high school, I got my hair colored for the first time. I had auburn streaks. My hair was just above my shoulders now, but you would think it was down my back based on the number of compliments I received. It was strange to me that it seemed like all I had to do was color my hair to not feel inadequate. I changed my hair color again and had my staple honey blonde all throughout junior and senior year. I thought it was cute and it really brightened my face in the summer. I was a teenager and didn't think much of it other than that. But a former track coach and teammates alluded to me wanting to be white because of my hair color and because I wasn't hanging with Black kids on the track team anymore. He claimed that some members of the track team were saying that soon I'd have blue eyes and blonde hair. All of this sounded stupid to me. I wasn't really close to any of them nor was there any beef. I was just always a low-key person. And besides, I quit the team after sophomore year, despite being one of the star runners on the team. I moved to the South Side and the commute for early morning practices was too much with two buses and a train ride. It was quite sad to me that a hair color, who you choose to hang with, and how you act could really make people think they can determine your Blackness for you.

I loved the honey blonde color and had no plans to remove it.

As time went on, I became more frustrated with Tom. It seemed like every appointment I scheduled with him he kept cutting my hair. I kept scheduling appointments with him for about six years at this point and was now a sophomore in college. I didn't go as much as I did when I was younger because I was able to maintain and grow my hair between relaxers. One day about a day or so after getting my usual relaxer, I combed my hair to find a lot of shedding – far more than normal. I instantly texted him and asked him what the heck was going on. I told him I became frustrated that every time I went to him for a relaxer, he would cut my hair more than requested. I guess guilt took hold of him because he confessed, he added the relaxer to my ends. This is an absolute NO for relaxing hair, and he knew that! He continued to confess that he didn't want to lose me as a client, which I guess would explain the excessive trimming and bad relaxer to keep me around. I was livid! Let's be real, I was beyond livid. I instantly started to plot a trip across town to do lord knows what that would have resulted in a felony. But after I calmed down, I started to think about how it would affect my family, my future, and the full scholarship I received for college. I just couldn't stoop to that level and go that route. He tried to keep apologizing, but I never responded and deleted his number. I never went back to him again. And I started to wonder how many other Tom's were out there ruining Black women's hair for a few dollars?

BRAIDS AND DAMAGED EDGES

I left the salon life for a while and decided to just get braids in my hair at this point. I just couldn't bear seeing my hair fall out again and going through that entire process. So, I decided letting my hair rest under braids would be best. I received a suggestion about a hair braiding shop to go to from a college friend, and I took off once again across the city to get my hair braided. I had been told I would basically be spending my entire day in the braid shop and that the braids would hurt terribly. I scheduled my appointment on a weekday, so I would have some time in the shop without a ton of people. I went to a lady who, until this day, I can't remember her name or what she looks like, but I do remember the nine hours in her chair getting my hair braided. I remember feeling like I was getting scalped every time she dug her fingers into my head to pull the braids tightly. My hair turned out beautifully! And although I could feel my scalp pulling apart every time I made a step forward, I knew it was all worth it. I took an Advil to numb the pain and continued with my day. I woke up the next day and my head was still killing me. The day after that it still hurt. It was just something I had to get used to. As they say, "beauty is pain". But at least I didn't have to worry about doing it. I figured whatever was happening underneath was better than fried, dyed, and damaged I'd endured with Tom. It was easy breezy from that standpoint. I actually really liked having my hair braided. At least for the first two weeks. I was told braids would last a least a month and was under the impression that when other women said it would last a month, that it would last a month in good shape. Well, that just wasn't the case for my hair. I could never get quite comfortable with washing and conditioning my hair with my braids still in. My 4C hair growing wildly underneath the braids just couldn't be kept tamed enough to keep the frizz away. I never did get those slick baby hair edges down either. No matter how many gel products I wasted money on, laying my edges never worked.

If getting my hair braided wasn't grueling and time-consuming enough, taking the braids out was also time-consuming. The process of cutting them, using rat tail combs to separate my natural hair from the fake hair, while trying not to damage my real hair was just a bit much for me. Especially having to ride across town to get new braids in and having to stuff my untamed hair under a baseball cap. It became a hassle pretty fast–not to mention costs. I had to bounce around a bit to different braiders because while I loved the first shop, my meager paychecks from Starbucks did not. Like any hairstyle, braids can be an investment. This was one that I got tired of pretty fast. After about six months I'd had enough, and I figured my hair had grown enough by then. So, I dropped the hair braiding altogether.

Taking my braids out for good was a bit scary. I had about six months of new growth and absolutely no idea what to do with it. Up until this point, I had been getting relaxers since I was six. I had no clue what I was doing with my new "Fredrick Douglas" hairdo and no intentions to learn. I remember standing in the mirror, getting frustrated trying to use my relaxer and braiding hair products on my newly natural hair. Now I know that was not a wise decision because there are different products for natural hair versus relaxed hair. But I had no choice but to use what was in my bathroom cabinet because I didn't quite think this whole process through. I had no hair appointments planned and was honing solely on my own skills, which were non-existent considering I had never had natural hair as an adult. I really should've thought this whole thing out.

After a mild attempt at straightening my hair, I quickly gave up and began looking for a new hair salon to flatten my curls. I found a place downtown, a few blocks from my dorm at the time. It was an Egyptian hair salon that was supposedly unmatched when it came to straightening and relaxing hair. I scheduled a consultation and gave them a run-down of my hair horror stories and how I was skeptical about getting a relaxer. He reassured me that everything would be okay and explained his whole process in detail. I scheduled an appointment. I was a bit nervous, but not too much. Everything seemed to go okay and I had no problems. I found a new salon to go to and my hair wasn't getting randomly cut and damaged this time.

Things were back to usual with my bimonthly relaxers. The new stylist I was going to really knew what he was doing and my hair was healthy and growing. But I got bored quickly and wanted something new. Sew-ins were getting pretty big on campus and I went ahead and fell in line with everyone else. Apparently, they were pretty easy to maintain. I went to a friend in college who did sew-ins for only sixty dollars. Her sew-in was really nice and she told me I'd love mine. It did look nice when it was done but trying to straighten my hair to match the fake hair was just too much for me. It also felt like a basket on my head and I hated not being able to actually scratch my scalp when it itched. The sew-in style did not last long. Only two weeks and I was completely over it. While the other girls in college loved it, my boyfriend, now husband, thought it looked ridiculous and preferred my relaxed hair or braids. Even one of my male friends told me when I went back to my normal self with my wrap that weave just wasn't me. I say this to say, it is interesting what women think some men want them to look like versus what they are okay with us looking like. This is up for debate though, as I think about most of the ridicule I received growing up coming from boys who preferred anything but. But this time as we got older, I guess perspectives changed and childish ways fade away.

I did notice the braiding and sew-ins seemed to be pulling back my edges a bit too much for my liking. And my hair in a certain area seemed to not be growing as fast, so I retired adding any kind of fake hair to my head altogether. Until this day, a portion of my edges in the center of my head has thinned due to the excessive center parts and hair pulling from the painful tight braids.

My then-boyfriend, who I think after a few years got sick of my frustrations and hair changes asked one day "why don't you just cut it all off and wear a fade?" I joked him off believing he couldn't possibly be serious, considering how hard I was trying to do the complete opposite. "No," he said. "I do actually think a short, natural style would look good on you." I did think about it for a minute, but I was way too invested in growing my hair and being a typical self-conscious college kid. It would only take me about a whole decade to realize that he was indeed right.

MY HALLE BERRY HAIRDO, AGAIN, AND THE ULTIMATE BIG CHOP

I went back to my wrap and did my hair myself for the most part. I would get relaxers occasionally, but not as much as I did before. My hair was growing, and it was healthy. I took the time to learn my head of hair and not depend on someone else to learn it for me. I didn't force my hair to look and be what it wasn't. But, one day I had enough of my hair. My hair grew but never quite went past my shoulders. I wanted to cut it, but not too much. My experience over the years made me afraid of how I would look. So, after a bad hair color that left my hair shedding terribly (the hair struggle just never seemed to end), I decided to cut my hair. I was out of college for a few years at this time and moved around the country a bit with my now husband's job. We landed right outside Detroit when I decided it was time for a change. I was finishing grad school and had landed my first job in marketing, which I had been trying to break into for a while. I wanted to feel like I was having a new beginning in a new location – starting my new career. I took a gamble on a Google search and came across a salon where I would become a regular customer for years to come. I got lucky on the first try, I guess. I called to schedule a consultation and showed up a few minutes early. I gave my whole hair spiel to her with a picture of the hairstyle I wanted. Two weeks later, I was rocking a short-tapered hairstyle, similar to the one I sported in grade school. Except, I was an adult now and it made sense! I would wear the short do and color my hair with my favorite honey blonde color.

I was working corporate at this time. I noticed the extra emphasis placed on how nice my tapered haircut was with honey blonde highlights. It made me think about my former track coach saying I would have blue eyes and blonde hair. I could not help but think that using the brighter hair color to add an extra "pop" and lighten up my face had something to do with how my White counterparts viewed me.

I remember walking into my supervisor's office after getting my hair colored the day before and she looked stunned and said "Oh wow, you look really nice. You should keep that color in your head." "Really?" I thought. I traveled a lot with my company doing events and selling our services. Image was important and keeping my short hairstyle with the honey blonde color was even more important because of this. While I loved the color, I felt the pressure to keep touching it up because I thought it looked appealing, after the compliments received at work. I hated knowing that I was placing this much emphasis on my hair, based on others' perception of me in the workplace.

I rocked my short and colored hairdo for about four years, but it became very costly and time-consuming to maintain. And while I loved the salon I went to, I couldn't help continuing to think about what my husband said about wearing a fade. I started preparing myself in the event that I did decide to do the big chop. I would slick my hair back occasionally, just to see how my hair would look, and constantly part and touch my scalp to check any random lumps or hair thinning – I did not want any surprises. I truly thought the big chop would actually suit me and be much more convenient, being that I have an active lifestyle. After a vacation in Belize and having to constantly co-wash and flat iron my hair while there, I decided once and for all to just chop it all off. I called my hairstylist and told her I needed to cut all my hair off. She was natural herself and told me to take a day or two to think about it because once it is gone, it is gone. But she did say she was happy I had gotten to this point of wearing my hair natural. I scheduled the appointment, went in, and chopped it all off with zero hesitation. I was not surprised by how I looked. I actually felt relieved. I'd done braids, a sew-in, color, and tapered cuts. I just wanted to feel free for once. I wanted to do a quick brush or wash and go and be done for the day. I didn't want to be tied down by my hair and other standards. I figured whatever opportunities didn't come my way, were just not meant to come my way. And whoever had an issue with my hair had to deal with that on their own terms – not mine.

I was happy with the results! I wanted my hair to look like it was styled and not like I just cut it off to grow it back again like I've seen many other women do. I did not want it to be some shameful experience. I've heard of many natural haired women doing the big chop and being distraught with it. They wanted to rush through to the big hair faze. I was in no rush for this! I wanted to own it and do so confidently. This confidence would carry on for a few days. I started going the textbook natural hair route, following suggestions from other people that just didn't work for my hair. And like everything else in life, trying to do it like everyone else didn't work for me. I went even further and did what just about every natural headed woman does when they have done the big chop – I went down the YouTube rabbit hole. I watched at least 100 videos, with all of the women using ten products just to get a few average curls. I have to admit it was a bit intimidating and discouraging. It seemed almost even more exhausting to follow these women's techniques for a fade than it was doing my long hair. Everyone was doing the same thing but they all obviously had different hair textures. It didn't seem like anyone even took the time to learn their hair, but just went with what they were told would work. Not to mention that in the natural hair community, it seemed like the desire for creating the mixed girl curl was more important than actually caring for the head of hair God blessed you with. It was frustrating. Many of these products didn't even work when I tried some of them with my relaxed hair, so I knew it wouldn't work with my natural hair.

After becoming a product junkie, buying any and every trendy product for natural hair, I had an epiphany to just go back to the basics of what my mother used for the few years that I did have natural hair. I stopped following trends and listened to my hair and figured out the products that worked best for it. These were many of the products that we've been told to steer clear of because they are not supposed to be good for our hair – hair grease, mineral oil, pomade for those edges, and a list of others. Those are what has worked for my hair and I don't even try to debate it. I did not try to force my hair to be what it wasn't. I have 4C hair and I embraced that.

I wore a fade for several years after and went to a barber for upkeep. I didn't feel tied down by my hair. I didn't have to worry about swimming, biking, hiking, or anything of the sort because I had a fade. I grew my hair out a bit recently and now have a TWA (Teeny Weeny Afro). I get my hair tapered at a barber every other week, color it every few months and I am good to go. I use a sponge daily to enhance my look. I don't overthink the natural hair process or follow the natural hair cult. I keep it simple and cute. One day I will rock an "Angela Davis" afro, but for now, the TWA will do.

Although I've had my ups and downs with my hair, I love my short, natural hair!

It's crazy how life comes full circle. What I got teased for as a kid (not having a lot of hair), is what I get complimented on all the time now. I wish I had the self-confidence to be natural much younger in life, but better later than never. I have my own business, so I haven't had the same setbacks as my other "naturalistas" working in Corporate America. And at this point, I have no desire to change my look to appeal to the masses because that is not my clientele. I know the journey is hard and not the same for us all, but natural hair is not a one-size-fits-all. I think it's best to just find a look that works for you naturally or not listen to your hair and take care of it accordingly. My hair is an extension of me. It no longer owns me. I own it and do so well.

8

My Crown Speaks

Mary E. May

I am midwestern, born and raised. Chi-town! I moved to the east coast, by way of Maryland/Washington DC, and then, shortly to Pennsylvania to complete an undergrad degree at an HBCU. I eventually accepted a job in the area after graduation. At this time, I found myself free from the personal hair prison I had developed from my childhood thanks to meeting my stylist, who cares for my hair to this day.

My hair perceptions developed very early on in my childhood. It was a combination of Midwestern flare along with southern Alabama influence that formed my personal hair journey. My parents came from two very different schools of thought when it came to cultural perspectives. My mother believed and valued a very Euro-centric refinement, rejecting most things related to the African American experience. Whereas my dad embraced a more inclusive ideology of melanated cultures and you could catch him at any given moment with his hair pick, you know the one, with the fist on the top. Naturally, my mom was the "unofficial stylist," and the preparation for hair washing day was always a challenge. A six-part process, this ongoing ordeal eventually caused me to question my beauty and Black image.

After Saturday activities, if it was a hair week, the day was all about hair until bedtime with several breaks in between for dinner and a shower. The process was sometimes broken into both weekend days due to fatigue of process for both of us. As I grew older, my mother who was of a seasoned age, grew weary of the painful hours that hair day consumed. She decided that my hair would benefit from a relaxer. I had no idea, at that time what that meant until the eight-hour process magically turned into two, minus the hot comb burns. Ouch! What neither of us knew was that this chemical would eventually send an internal message that my hair in its natural state was not good enough. After the change, something inherently felt different with the hair God had given me. This was not just the silent message sent through my mom's actions of putting a perm in my hair, it was a message that was woven through the messages I received from the rest of the women in my family as well. There seemed to be few positive affirmations for me that could have built healthy self-esteem and love for self. Instead, I was subjected to negative remarks as they pertained to my hair every Sunday.

Sundays would start with us attending service at church. During Sunday service, I would receive compliments that boosted my energy and a radiant smile, but that would change as we set out on that fifteen minute drive to my grandmothers' house for our Sunday family dinner. During the short drive, I would begin to hug myself out of anxiety, because I never knew what comments would be coming my way. This tradition of family dinner did nothing to build my esteem, character, and love that I received elsewhere.

On many occasions, I tried to ask for invitations to go with other church member's families after service or to even visit with my father to avoid the energy that would be present at my grand-mother's house. Yet, to no avail, I was back at the same place I somewhat dreaded every Sunday. Sometimes it worked and other times it did not. I would continue to walk into the house referred to as 400 West, high as a kite with anxiety. Initial greetings by the family were affirming and complimentary. However, as I made my way to the kitchen where our matriarch stood, she would begin her examination of me from head to toe a few times before she formulated her actual greeting. She appraised what I wore to church before she started on my hair. When her gaze made it to the top of my head, her comments were never approving.

Additionally, because my hair was naturally thick and long compared to my grandmother's, her comments walked the line of being condescending since I did not have what she believed to be beautiful hair. The conversation would last for ten minutes, yet it seemed like an eternity. Throughout the day, she would revisit my hair every time I came within her eyesight. I would attempt to avoid my grandmother at all costs, which became easier as more family members arrived for Sunday dinner. After enjoying the meal, I would check in with my mother every so often to ask when we were leaving in hopes that we would not visit again until the next Sunday's dinner.

As I developed into a young adolescent, my hair and personal appearance became more important. The more active I became, the more interested I became in the manageability of my hair. It was important to maintain my style while keeping myself neat and fashionable. Unfortunately, my grandmother thought dif-ferently. I was told that I was being "too sassy and grown" and "not in a teenager's place," because I had chosen to exhibit some independence with my hair and required little to no help. In her language, I must have been "fresh and sassy." This shocked me because my intention and focus were the total opposite. This new set of insults were compound with the ongoing family debates of who had the better grade of hair during dinners at her house. All of this seemed dumb to me and appeared to have no purpose, and unfortunately, no end. Sadly, this didn't help me to understand who I was nor who I would become.

During my middle school years, we moved into my grandmother's home where I was exposed to critical antics daily. In a sense, the negative comments of me were also aimed at my mother for how my hairstyling was done. My image was never approved by my grandmother.

In high school, I often asked my mother if I could cut my hair. She stood her ground, and every time that I asked, her answer was no. Finally, one day I shared that I would pay to have my hair cut by a professional. Her response was I could do whatever I wanted when I could pay for it. Yes! The seed was officially planted. I could finally fashion my hair how I wanted it to be. My musical influence of Janet Jackson, Michael Jackson, Prince, Cyndi Lauper, Pat Benatar, Morris Day, and Whitney Houston had me longing for all types of fun and sassy hair, I couldn't wait! As I prepared for my fifteenth birthday party, my mother was playing a competitive BRIDGE game in a local Marriott. She asked me to come into the banquet hall to show her my hair when I returned to the hotel, which was where my party would later be held. I strutted confidently into the room with a new sense of freedom. I had cut my hair and I was rocking a new sassy style! My mother's facial expression was priceless. Although I received multiple compliments from the other ladies, my mother's facial expression was frozen in disbelief. I had finally done it; I had cut my hair and I was beaming from ear to ear!

Our battle about how my hair represented me from this point forward always became a source of disagreement. It was a challenge that I welcomed with no problem because after all, it was my hair and not hers. The journey of rejection, acceptance, and confidence was a bumpy one. Seeking to understand and reconcile rejection, the survival of self, and how I fit in became the norm that I sought to disrupt. My hair was not only a part of me, it was the outside expression of how I wanted to represent myself in the absence of seeking approval, love, affirmation, and value from the surface, texture, and style of my hair.

My hair transition in my college years at the HBCU I attended was by choice. It was a short and sassy "Halle Berry" bob, which was everything to me. In the college setting, the narrative was different when it came to Black hair. The social conversations of faculty and students represented varying backgrounds that evolved around their sense of culture, fashion, and Black pride. I found these conversations refreshing.

At a certain point, I decided that managing my own hair was not my desire and I needed to make some decisions around selecting a stylist. I began to observe, and interview who would be the best match for me and provide the best experience for my hair care. I asked about their self-care practices regarding their hair, making sure the person I selected would be the best fit for me. Once I decided on a stylist, after every appointment, after the mirror head nod review, I quickly inquired about how to keep that particular look. These styles consisted of the sassy bob, finger waves, and other early nineties hairstyles. My hair remained healthy, strong, and resilient, despite the chemicals. My concern was about my forehead being big and that my styles needed to cover and shape my face; however, my trusted stylist groomed me out of that thought process. Unfortunately, my family had deposited this negative perception into me when they would discuss my hair. The view in the mirror was often challenged by the negative voices from my past.

As an emerging adult, my hair chronicles continued to evolve while living on the East coast. At this time I had been employed by multiple African American-owned establishments where hair was a part of the status checklist. This status checklist also included social class, sorority membership, and other social connections. It was also a part of office politics as well. The debates would become intense around a variety of concerns. Those discussions dealt with the latest fashions and if the creamy crack was even necessary to use on your hair. This part directly related to me and my choices. In these cases, my midwestern upbringing, values, and beliefs were always challenged and misunderstood. However, I was a full member of the creamy crack team and that would be noted that I was damaging my hair and also the culture.

Eventually, a health scare and medication change shifted the chemistry of my hair, but with the help of a nurturing stylist and communication about what was going on with me outside of my hair, she was able to give me the maintenance, love, and care needed during that transition. I was consistent in my hair care routine, making sure that the same set of healthy hands were always monitoring the strength and integrity of my hair. This interruption with my health did not impact nor disrupt my hair remaining healthy.

As my journey continued, my hair remained resilient and strong even while continuing to use relaxers. In my mind, I praised perms. I celebrated my hair appointment day, which I secretly called *Creamy Crack Day*. This day meant manageability of my hair and more time to snooze in the mornings. Chemical relaxers also allowed me to meet the standards of the corporate appearance and costume I was expected to maintain for my nine to five.

My boss and colleagues valued big hair and expensive weaves that ranged from three hundred to seven hundred dollars for bundles of hair. This was a very foreign experience to me since I'd always had healthy hair that was also always a good length. I did not question their choice, yet they questioned and challenged mine each and every time. The mindset of this type of investment in hair was bewildering and seemed so unrealistic to me. I couldn't believe people invested so much money into changing their appearance. I thought of it as being a contradiction of self.

Along with the contradiction of self, my mindset focused on the reality that my basic needs were a thousand dollars in rent, utilities, car note, and insurance which were more important than buying a thousand dollars worth of hair bundles. Do not get it twisted, I definitely believe in self-care; however, at that time, my line item in my budget did not extend past one hundred dollars to one hundred and forty dollars per month for my fashionable hair stylings. I was okay with being the outcast of that group. Yet, the debates with my boss resembled the debates I once had with my mother. The difference was now the inclusion of a corporate/business brand. It also seemed like a false identity of who I was as a person. At the same time, I was developing my 'why' for my business name to be inclusive of a butterfly and love of self from the inside out. The two worlds no longer made sense together.

Several years later, my hairstylist pointed out that the amount of heat I was using on my hair was becoming an issue. Therefore, the conversation of protecting my hair so it could remain healthy, meant I had to embrace some form of protective style or a natural transition needed to take place. Initially, I went with not so "good" store-bought hair because it was easily accessible for protective styles. I enjoyed the new freedom and creativity from crochet weaves to sew-ins with color and versatility.

Even in preparing for family holidays or visits with family, I had to make sure that my costume was perfect. I would manage my hair care around those times very closely so that the style I chose could be as fresh as butter and be within their approval. Upon arriving, both of my parents would glance me over from head to toe, before settling on my head. If my mother were at arm's length, I would be prepared to duck as she would want to touch my hair. My glance would be quick. You do not touch a Black woman's head of hair! My father would have this discerning look, totaling me up and letting me know what he approved of and what he did not. Because I knew it was coming, I would plan my attire for the entire visit to ensure that I would pass their appraisal, while staying in alignment with what I liked.

As I strive to always represent the authentic me, I've learned that it is important to be a representative of more than just my hair. Yes, my hair shapes my perception, but it is not all of me. In the business culture, wearing the costume that 'closes the deal' compromises who I truly want to represent. As I receive requests for media interviews, my default thought before my "yes" is what does my crown, my hair represent today. This will shape if I feel able to say yes or no, especially since the time frame of an invitation is within hours–up to–a day before filming. In talking with colleagues that share similar platforms, it became obvious that we had the same challenges. The hair conversation in the business culture and setting includes making your costumes match with your audience. The narrative around the branding of my skills, outfit, and content that I bring to the conversation becomes secondary to my hair. There should be no debate about how a woman chooses to style and represent herself. Just like her attire, her hair is a part of her journey.

My crown remains healthy even with the seasoning of grey around my hairline. I embrace my hair because it represents who I am. I am a greater giant in my work and integrity because of my awareness of self, which includes my hair. I understand that perceptions about one's hair are instrumental parts of your core and shapes how you manage other areas of your life and relationships. If someone were to challenge my choices, I now simply disrupt their narrative, which is usually filled with stereotypes, and bring them back to the reality of me. Embracing the fact that my perception, journey, and perspective is not determined by someone else's experience has served me well.

9

Stop Running From DreadLocks

Ieisha Fuller

*E*ither the hot, humid weather or random rain occurrences has turned my pressed tresses into woolly messes on many occasions. These are the expectations of black hair in the South; however, managing the expectations of others as it pertains to MY hair was a new experience for me to navigate while working in higher education. I had never been approached so many times with questions to touch it, inquiries as to if it is mine, or "What are you doing with it?" in my entire life, until I arrived at this predominantly white institution, better known as a PWI. The irony in all of this was, this wasn't my first time working in this type of environment, but for some reason this situation was extremely different.

I began working at the institution part time, but after several months and after completing my Bachelors Degree, I was encouraged to apply for another position and was hired to work full time as an administrative assistant. The irony of the promotion involved me transitioning from part time to a full time role, which occasionally included me working on the weekends. I was excited for this new experience, as well as the new income, but I hadn't fully assessed how much this new position would really cost me. As the responsibility of being an administrative assistant became very heavy and the time commitments increased, the responsibilities of my home life quickly began to suffer and I knew something had to change. Oh and by the way did I mention, I was a single mother of two young children?

As I began weighing my options for change, I realized I needed to assess what could come off my plate and start saving me some time. Of course, of all the things I considered, my hair was at the top of the list. I had been considering for a long time transitioning my hair to locs, also known as dreads or dreadlocks, which the last two of the terms I despise only because of the negative connotation. However in my considering this transition, there never seemed to be a *RIGHT* time! I'd transitioned to natural hair in my early twenties, but was having trouble with the daily maintenance of my curly coils. As I quickly learned, natural hair requires a huge time commitment. I started over every morning, as my pillow turned into some sort of vacuum and sucked all the moisture from my hair while I slept; returning my hair to its product-less wooly state. After consistently losing this battle, with the help of the Dominican salon, I decided to revert back to the European look but without the creamy crack better known as a perm. This was a whole new level that I had heard about, but *knew* nothing about, until I actually signed up for this level of commitment to my haircare.

Now, the good thing about the Dominican salon was 1) it was cheaper and 2) it cut my hair maintenance time in half. After my first trip to a Dominican salon, I understood first hand why it took half the time. When I arrived, a young lady greeted me and quickly ushered me to the shampoo bowl where she washed and conditioned my hair. Then she applied a really nice soothing hydration treatment and placed me under this little steamer like machine for a few minutes. When the treatment was done, I was directed to a styling chair and then this is where things went left. She grabbed what appeared to be a blow dryer and a rounded brush. The reason I say appeared to be a blow dryer is because when she turned it on, THE AMOUNT OF HEAT that came out of that dryer was absolutely abusive. It should be illegal for a hair dryer manufacturer to be allowed to produce a machine that generates that much heat to be projected directly to a person's head or brain for *any* length of time, let alone up to twenty minutes. She moved what I considered to be a mini blow torch through my head with her rounded metal spiky brush, creating enough static that I was sure I could pick up cable. She brushed, pulled, blew and yanked my head in every direction as she made sure every inch was dry. All I could think is what in the world had I gotten myself into. I wanted to cry. Then as if the dryer wasn't enough, she pulled out the flat irons that I am sure could only be manufactured in hell, she sectioned off my hair and placed it between the plates of those flat irons. You really cannot understand that those plates from hell were literally millimeters away from either my ear, forehead, or nape of neck being scarred for life. All of this in pursuit of the silky look of perfection, really?!!!!! When I left the salon the silky look of perfection *was* achieved, but my head was on fire and I dare not add water otherwise my hair would return to its pre-tamed state. But was this what I was going to have to endure?

Reluctantly I continued this method of torture for several more weeks as I convinced myself that all was well. This was a small sacrifice to help me save both time and money. Nevertheless, I was intensely in pursuit of other alternatives and could not escape the nagging desire to transition my hair to locs. I just felt locs were the answer. However, as I mentioned earlier, I was a new administrative assistant in higher education at a PWI and to say that I was a bit uncomfortable about what this transition would mean would be an understatement. As an administrative assistant in this particular environment (although it may not have ever been said directly), you are a representative of the person you support. You needed to look a certain way and carry yourself in a certain way in order to be perceived as effective. Now the pressed look was how I had been hired, but in my mind the loc'd look was going to allow me the sanity to maintain my job. Even as I am recounting this story, the financial struggle associated with the decisions and sacrifices necessary just to be employed as a young Black single mother pains me. As a Black woman, I found myself always trying to compete in the environment of other races while always over performing, while being underfunded. You may be asking what I mean by that, so let me share the economics of job, hair, and environment with you.

When I was hired, I came to the job with fifteen years of administrative level experience, including billing, coding, veterinary services, government, non profit and other institutions. However, when I was promoted full time, I didn't realize that my income actually went down, instead of increasing. Now some may say that was my fault for not knowing my worth and value, but as I had watched so many other Black women with degrees in the environment be overlooked for promotions or only finding solace in leaving, I couldn't allow myself to think in that way. I had two small children, and this job was supposed to provide the stability that everyone told me as a single mom, I needed to have. However, I also saw the path of working as an administrative assistant a limited one, where a lot of people who looked like me were all competing for that limited, almost non-existent, but coveted title of Office Manager too, and I was no different. Luckily, being naive, (and I think he knew it) I had a supervisor who I felt did some negotiating on my behalf for which I was forever grateful. Once I got into the role, I realized there was a lot more to this job than administrative work and that's an entirely different story..., however even with the negotiating done by my supervisor, the ends did not meet my needs. My benefits cost more, the weekend commitments were impeding on my family time, and the administrative timelines were overwhelming. Yes it appeared that I received more, but the income did not equate to the outcome. To give you an example, as it related to my hair care at the time, for general hair maintenance, I was easily paying eighty-five dollars and that was without leaving a tip. Of course with a tip and twice a month maintenance, my bill came to $180/month and approximately sixteen hours of my life spent at the salon. Now if you recall, I mentioned this job included some weekend events, which I was required to attend. So then the issue became, when was I supposed to spend sixteen hours in the salon, not to mention, raise my children? Now to some $180/month on hair may not seem like a lot, but for a single mother of two, counting every coin was a necessity, especially considering that $180 did not include my son or my daughter's hair maintenance and time commitment. In contemplating the changes I wanted to make to my hair, I was sensitive to the potential backlash I may have received and I needed to be sure I was ready.

As I began transitioning from one stylist to another, trying to find that perfect person who would consistently remain within my budget while still maintaining a certain quality of care, I was finally introduced to Nae. Nae was a young lady who moved from Pennsylvania to Georgia, and she had a true hand for natural hair. When I met Nae she began transitioning my weave infused braids to my own natural hair through braided styles. This transition alone was huge for me. I've always had A LOT of hair, but it was just customary for braiders to tell me how many packs of hair I would need for a style. Well when I met Nae, one of the first things she asked was, "Why do you need to add hair?" I looked at her kind of crazy and thought to myself, "Does she really know how to braid hair?!." I had never had anyone ask me something like that before, so I asked her, "Do you mean you can braid my hair just like this?" She said, "Of course." I was blown away, she reminded me that the braids may not be as long, but the styles she created were unbelievable. With my newfound natural hair stylist, my hair began to grow even more and I began to celebrate my natural hair. Yes, I was in love—with my own hair! However, it wasn't long before the hair cost and time commitment started to become an issue yet again. As my hair grew it began to require more time to style; more time equalled a higher the cost. There was no way I was going looking for yet another stylist. So I decided to explore the idea with Nae about my nagging desire to transition to locs. Nae, in true Nae fashion was like, "of course, you can do it!" We discussed the idea during a few more visits, before she debunked yet another myth.

Among other things, the concern of cutting my hair to transition to locs was a little nerve racking for me. We had spent all this time growing my hair just to cut it off? I wasn't ready for that. Besides, if I cut my hair and started the locs in the traditional look, everyone at work would know which caused me to wonder if I would lose my job. Again, Nae settled my concerns. She explained, I did not have to cut my hair in order to start locs. She told me when I was ready she would simply start them as double strand twists which would allow me to keep my length. Nae successfully calmed my concern of how we would start them, but I still had the nagging concern of how will my job react?

For people of other cultures, the thought of making hair transitions such as a cut, color, bald, trim, beard, etc are not of concern except maybe in obviously more conservative fields like banking or law. However, to be a Black female administrative assistant at a PWI-trust me, I had received enough comments to put me on alert. These comments would be any of which went beyond my hair, so I was well aware this transition would be noticed. Oftentimes, it was from other African American women who were "looking out for me." Needless to say, I was worried if I made this transition to locs I would lose my job. I decided I would have to find out.

Nae started my locs as two strand twists which just as she promised, served as somewhat of a camouflage. I kept them wrapped in a scarf, when I wasn't at work doing very little to them to allow the locs to form. As my locs matured, I began putting bows in my hair to decorate the styles and lower suspicion. However, it was still interesting how much conversation and attention this simple change of my hair received. People would compare me to this person or that person which oftentimes the person they referenced did not have the most flattering appeal to a Black woman in the South. I just kept thinking, "What is all this concern over my hair especially without understanding the why." Yes, part of the transition was I wanted locs; however the bigger desired outcome was needing to make a transition to juggle the many other time consuming tasks of job, home and raising children. As a matter of fact, my children have their own hair story intertwined.

In having a daughter and son (eighteen months apart), Sunday had become hair day in our house while dinner was either cooking in the crock pot, oven or on the stove. In between stirring or checking the oven, I was cutting my son's hair or blow drying and styling my daughter's hair for the coming week. My daughter had a head full of hair, too and I didn't have Saturdays to give to a hair salon for me let alone both of us. Because just as I was being judged I had to make sure that my children were not being judged.

The emphasis we place on hair is astonishing to me because it is not only by other cultures, but within our own culture as well. I remember one year, my son was in elementary school and it was awards day. He had gotten all dressed up in his suit and I had picked out his hair as he was in between haircuts, but you could not tell him he did not look handsome. Again, I was so proud of him for his grades and accolades for the semester, his lack of a haircut was irrelevant or so I thought. I had gone through the day, celebrated my son, taken pictures and was truly proud of him. Then I posted the pictures on social media. Why did I do that? Of course, there were the celebratory comments, but someone actually had the nerve to post something negative. Then had the audacity to follow it up with a phone call to ask me why hadn't I gotten my son's haircut. I LOST IT! I CUSSED him flat out! Not only was I managing my own hair journey as it related to career, but the nerve of this random man to say something to me about why my son's hair wasn't cut. Why wasn't the conversation, "do you mind if I stop by and take your son to get a haircut to celebrate his accomplishment?" As I think back to that moment, it continues to amaze me how narrow minded our focus is at times. My son's accomplishments had been totally overshadowed by someone else's concern over his hair. Meanwhile at my job, my story wasn't much different.

Since people didn't exactly know I was transitioning to locs, I remember hearing or being in the midst of conversations with people saying, "I hope you're not getting ready to do locs" or "I am glad you are not doing locs. You know, I can't stand to see people with those things because she or he looks so dirty or unkempt." Again, I kept wondering, why are people so concerned about my hair? Why wasn't this the same sentiment shared when white women showed up to work with their hair dripping wet straight out the shower? I mean just because you added water did you think I want you dripping your wet hair all over me or my desk? I was more concerned with why I was not being paid a fair wage so I could show up just like everyone else did while being able to do whatever I want with my hair. How often do Black women neglect the costs and time that goes into not only our hair and other general maintenance when we go into a career environment? I know I didn't. There are costs to consider that contribute to your worth and value, which are needed to show up fully at a job and I believe many times we underestimate that need.

Locs became my way of being able to financially sustain working and doing something with my hair that I would allow for what I deemed a presentable look at work. The journey to locs provided me insight to the difference in how some people saw us not only in a PWI as well as how we saw ourselves. I remember thinking a lot of the scholars or women of wisdom I looked up to such as Angela Davis, Toni Morrison and Lauren Hill had either natural hair or locs. So to hear white and even some Black women say that the look made us look unkempt and dirty went against what I admired about some of our most accomplished and transformational women of the culture. To know that these women who I celebrated as graceful, wise, insightful and accomplished may have been thought of as dirty and unkempt? These conversations really opened my eyes to how we are constantly judged on things often beyond our control, but even deeper than that, constantly judged or critiqued for being just who we are. As a single Black woman with children, going into the workplace I came to understand the time, value and added costs associated with our routine maintenance and basic necessities are built on a flawed blueprint. I was told to go to school, get a job, get a degree or three which lands many of us in so much debt that we are forever digging ourselves out of that issue. Then we compound the debt, while living out the "fake it until you make it" principle. Then after you achieve all of that, the ever coveted salaried position which ends up to the equivalent of minimum wage once inflation is taken into account. As I navigated this new found reality, I realized I needed to accept it for what it was and get out of it what I needed, and help as many as I could along the way. My mission at the university became less about the institution and more about how I could help generations move through this space with a better sense of awareness. I hoped that by wearing my locs, I would be seen by students as someone with wounds, wisdom and grace who could be a guide to help them navigate what the classroom of these institutions would not.

After reading this, I am sure many people are saying why would you continue to stay in a place where you obviously felt so undervalued? When you have children, you realize it is truly no longer about you, BUT every decision YOU make impacts them. Besides where could I go where my hair wouldn't follow me or where small minded people would continue to project their judgement on me as well as on my children? Transitioning my hair was not only a big deal for me but it impacted my children, which because of social media, does not seem to get a pass.

I remember a while back, Beyonce's daughter was captured in a picture as a child with free flowing hair. The backlash of people stating how Beyonce' shouldn't let her daughter walk around like that or she should have had her hair done for the photo shoot was truly astounding. Here's a married, Black woman at billionaire status, sharing pics of her daughter being a child and society still had something to say? If Beyonce couldn't catch a break, then how could I expect to catch one. With that reality check, I realized just how much I needed to be on top of my daughter's hair and image even if I needed to let mine suffer to do so. The other reality check that came from the shaming of Beyonce regarding her daughter's hair, affirming for me the feeling of shame or guilt I sometimes felt taking my children to certain places, if it was an "off" week for hair care or general maintenance. This was especially difficult around family members who before they could say hello, would first comment about my daughter's hair or say to my son, boy you need a haircut. Knowing that the children had no control over their hair. I took that as a personal jab and felt even more belittled. First, from the job and now from family. Where was the support? The reality was the longer I was working, the more behind I began to feel. Even though I was cutting every unnecessary expense, it just didn't seem to be enough and would always come down to how do you maintain their hair? My son didn't seem to care as much but my daughter heard how everyone made hair such a big deal. I definitely think it took a toll on her in middle school and continues to take a toll. Like I said, family can do a number on you as well, and although I am sure they mean well, you are not always in a place mentally to hear what they have to say. As a matter of fact, I remember my aunt saying to me, "um, you know, I'm not telling you how to raise your kids or anything like that, but I know you need to get her hair done." She was referring to my daughter. Now my aunt was the type of woman that if she said something about anything, she was going to get in the issue with you to do something about it rather than just make idle conversation. What my aunt didn't know was I was in school for a Paralegal studies program, hoping to improve my job opportunities, that was meeting from nine a.m.–four p.m. on Saturdays. Of course with having class all day on Saturday, haircare day moved back to Sunday. Now my aunt was a married stay at home mom when she had children. She decided to return to work as a substitute teacher when her children were grown and in college. She was not making a lot of money, however true to who she is, since she spoke on the issue she decided she was going to help especially when she realized I was in school. She told me, "I am going to set aside fifty dollars every two weeks for you for your daughter's hair." Now little did I know at the time she was battling her own health issues, but I hadn't planned on following up with her about the money. However, the irony was as her health challenges evolved, she showed me just how dedicated she was to making sure that those funds were in place for my daughter. She would call every two weeks and either drop the money by the house or call me with some random reason to stop by the house to give me the money. So imagine this woman becoming ever so frail, getting behind the wheel of this 2003 Ford Explorer going to work as a substitute teacher, battling cancer, losing her own hair; setting aside fifty dollars to make sure my daughter's hair was taken care of. I truly came to understand just how much we are judged on our hair and what it meant to my aunt to make sure that judgment did not befall on my child.

Proudly, I am still wearing my locs almost ten years later and I didn't lose my job. The transition was the best decision I could have made for me and my family. There are days when I want to cut them, days where they are styled perfectly, and days when I just let my hair do what it does. With my locs, I have found a sense of confidence that pulls me through the bad hair days as I continue to embrace the "I am not my hair, but it is a *part* of me" journey. There are days along this journey when I may be a little self conscious if I wasn't able to get my locs done right before a picture or an interview, so they may not be as tight as I would like them to appear. However, I don't let it bother me.

Do I think my career options may have suffered, because of the choices with my hair? Maybe, but I don't know. What I do know is it allowed me to accept that some people are going to like you and some people are not. If those that don't like me, chose not to like me because of my hair rather than get to know me, then I haven't missed a thing. I realize navigating my own mind is more than enough. I don't have time nor is it my job to navigate the minds of others if it is not an even exchange. My goal at this point is to keep as much of my hair on my head as I choose. If I decide to cut it, that's my choice. If I decide to straighten it, that's my choice. If I decide to color it, that's also my choice. I think the one superpower that is often overlooked is our power of choice, even for something as simple as our hair!

10

The Soul That Lives Within

Carmela Fisher, LCPC

*I*n 2006, India Arie came out with a song titled, "*I Am Not My Hair*," which gave a chronological account of the ups and downs the artist faced with her hair throughout her life. The song ends with her finally coming to terms with how society views Black women and their hair and how she ultimately embraced her own kinky, curly, tress and crown. Yes, that song was a Black woman's "National Hair Anthem." I remember it vividly, as I pumped it in my car for months because I, too, could relate to the lyrics and challenges the artist faced. This was also the year I graduated from Towson University 's graduate program, a predominantly white college in Maryland. At that time, I was contemplating whether I would wear my hair natural, texturized or continue getting it relaxed before entering into the corporate world and trying to stay professional without "offending" the masses. Some refer to this as culturally accommodating and assimilating. Either way, I was uncomfortable with my hair's identity for well over three and a half years. As I write this, I hold a license in both Cosmetology and Mental Health. I realize my hair is a way I express myself. To date, I would also have you know I have been relaxer free for ten years now and will profess to anyone that "I am not my hair, but I am more than my hair… I am the soul that lives within." Now, sit back and relax, as I share with you my hair story.

As a young girl, maybe eight or so, I can recall those daunting "Easter Sunday" hairdos. It was always the night before Easter as I sit here begrudgingly reminiscing, I was placed in between my momma's legs getting my hair pressed and curled with that infamous hot straightening comb. Momma was always promising not to burn me, but it was never reassuring because she managed to burn me every time. It was the extreme heat that somehow kissed the back of my neck as it was evident from the scab that was present from the last time momma did my hair. Man oh man, did I hate that experience because my hair was so thin and fine. At any rate, momma would always prep my hair for pressing with the Dax hair grease, a green or blue hair grease which was infused with the pungent Bergamot smell, which guaranteed to give you longer and thicker hair in no time-but not my hair! After the straightening, came the croquignole curls (also known as ringlets or the Shirley Temple curls). To help make the curls set in and further hold the hair in place. Momma would protect my style with the pink sponge rollers to help reinforce those tight curls. Then, she would tie my hair down with a satin scarf so tight that it left a huge imprint on my forehead. Well, that satin scarf also made my hair sweat and it would eventually come off. But I would still have those rollers on lock, which managed to leave a print on my hair. Yes, it was a disaster. Whew-chile! Come Easter Sunday, we would take our pictures, and my hair would always revert back to its normal state within two hours and all you could smell was my burnt hair, mixed with that Bergamot. Yuck!

Momma and I always fought about my hair and the many different transitions it went through, even as an adult (braided styles, Jheri Curls, relaxers, hair additions, wigs and scarves). I totally abhorred my hair because I felt it had a personality of its own. I called my hair Cam, as I identified it to my alter-Sh-ego, which was at that time; very thin, brown, fine- textured, with little density. Anytime you would see my hair, it always reverted back to its original state making it challenging for any stylist to deal with. For years, my hair made me feel insecure and unattractive and I was often criticized about it. I often wondered whoever said, "A woman's hair is her crown and glory," was obviously not living in my shoes because my hair felt far from that truth. I felt like I was cursed and could never find my crown.

One pivotal point in my hair story came around the age of twelve, when my cousin whose hair and personality happened to be the total opposite mine, came to visit. Our differences were not bad, and I found it enlightening because we are like Yin and Yang. I was the extrovert and she is the introvert. I was a "tomboy" and she was a "girly-girl." Many people often said we looked alike, but the noticeable difference was our hair. Her hair was the opposite of mine, long, thick, and black and you could do anything with it. Ironically, she didn't like her hair and was often teased about it growing up. Well, we decided to visit my grandmother's house which was down the street from where I lived. On this particular day, my grandfather (affectionately known as Haus), was home. Haus was seldom home because he worked all the time, and if he was home, many knew he was a man of little words. When he spoke, it was brief unless he was telling you this joke: "If M-U-L-Y spells muly-What does J-U-L-Y spell?" However, on this day, there was no joke. My grandfather turned directly to my cousin and said, "You got some pretty hair!" I'd never heard my grandfather say much to anyone; nevertheless, give them a compliment. Wouldn't you know, those words he said to her paralyzed me, and I held on to that experience unconsciously for quite a long time until it came up while I was engaging in my own mental health recovery. I totally admire my cousin and was never jealous or envious of the blessings God had given her. However, I do know I was looking to be acknowledged or complimented by my own grandfather, but I soon came to terms with the fact that would never happen.

After that day, I started doing my own hair and if/when I burned it, I took responsibility for my mistakes. What I also learned was my creativity was free flowing and unlimited. People began to constantly compliment me on my hair. So much so, I started doing a lot of the younger girl's hair in the neighborhood. After completing high school, I decided I would go to cosmetology school and hone in on my craft of creating hairstyles to compliment personalities. While in cosmetology school, I recall listening to many of the Black women sitting in my chair who had similar stories about their hair while growing up. Mind you, this was long before the natural hair phenomenon that we are seeing today. What I noticed was their hair was not their crown and glory either. It was amazing to see and hear that other women felt tormented about their hair and the process they went through while growing up. We often shared and compared our stories. When they sat in my chair, I could relate to them while making them look and feel pretty darn good in the process.

One story, I recall, was when a young lady from the Carolina's came to the school to get her hair done. She talked about how she would often go to the salon and get her hair done for Easter and her stylist said she was so stressed that she was thinning in the crown of hair; further emphasizing, she did not think anything about it because she was under a tremendous amount of stress. Then once, while she was getting her hair done, she happened to look in the mirror. That's when she saw her stylist performing a "pocket curl. I asked, "What is a pocket curl?" She replied, "It's when a person burns your hair and sticks the curl in their pocket. Not only did she have hair troubles, she also developed trust issues with women. Needless to say, I am so glad to have earned her trust in both areas.

Consequently, I was not earning a lot of money doing hair at this time because I didn't truly know the business side nor how to monetize properly and wanted to step away from doing hair for a while. That's when I decided to enlist into the US Army to change the pace a little and define or redefine my life in this hair business. I continued my hair journey even after I enlisted in the military and was stationed in Hawaii.

You see, the military was notorious for telling women, and particularly Black women, how they should wear their hair. Yes, you guessed it, those restrictions did not serve me well because I knew a person's hair was tied to their personality/identity and I needed to remain artistically expressive. I did not like the fact that I could only wear my hair in certain styles most of the time. Therefore, I only completed one term of enlistment and decided to stay in North Carolina and continue on the hair journey.

In North Carolina, I worked at Wave Links Hair Studios, a salon with some of the most talented platform hair artists in the industry. It was a beautiful time in my life and I was finally learning to do a lot of things with my hair as well as with my clients hair. I decided to go back to school and learn the business side of Cosmetology so I could do more. It was a beautiful process and I enjoyed the journey. I was doing door to door sales and teaching people how to style and maintain their hair at home when they were not able to come into the salon. It was an amazing time! However, two years later my life would take a radical turn: Personally, I was going through a divorce; physically I had multiple medical concerns; and financially I had filed bankruptcy. I had to put the world of Cosmetology on hold and relocated back to Maryland to care for my father who had taken ill during this time.

While in Maryland, I had to get myself and family acclimated to the new changes. I put off doing hair for a few months due to some physical challenges and I still wanted to learn more about business. As such, I began working as an Administrative Assistance at a mortgage lending company in order to have medical benefits for me and my children. The job offered limited compensation with a marginal benefits package, but the perks were amazing. They provided sky-boxed tickets to all the sporting events in town, which my family and I truly enjoyed. As you would imagine, the staff was diverse ethnically and racially, but it was primarily operated by a Jewish community. This was another one of the most challenging times in my hair story. I remembered my supervisor, a Jewish woman, telling me I dressed "too flamboyant" and it did not serve the company well. She even gave me a negative performance rating and told me to start wearing khakis and a polo shirt. One day, I canvassed the workplace and to my surprise, the only person(s) wearing khakis were the men. I became perplexed as to why she would try to have me dull my appearance when all the other women did not dress as such. That's when I told her, "You don't even wear khakis!" The atmosphere became a little strained afterwards. I knew she was not addressing my clothes at all. It was my hair that was always styled nicely and most of my co-workers looked forward to seeing what style I would come in with next. In retrospect, it was this same supervisor who had me cut her son's hair on the job. Can you believe that? Now, as you can imagine, the sister came to work dressed, but after this encounter, I was going to show her. As fate would have it, the company laid me off a few months later and provided me a decent severance package. The day I left, I walked out of there looking like I was on the cover of a fiction novel which read, "Ain't Nobody Business But My Own," with my hair finger-waved in a high beehive and nice colorful red, canary yellow and orange two-piece suit. As far as I remember, I was never told that I was overly dressed again.

God saw something better for me. He sent me back to school to a historically Black college, Morgan State University, to study Psychology. My entire time at Morgan, I had a sense of identity about myself. My hair was never an issue the entire time there. It was like I was in a land of Black utopia. There was a certain richness about my people and my culture, and I loved every moment of it. No matter how I wore my hair or how fashionably expressive my dressing, I owned my appearance and everything about me with dignity and pride. After undergraduate studies, I decided to further my education in the field of psychology. As such, I enrolled at Towson University in their Counseling Psychology program and things truly began to change. For starters, there was a difference in the climate as it was a predominantly white college. The way in which students treat you was totally different from the HBCU I had attended. At Towson, you were identified by a number; whereas, at Morgan, students were personally identified by name. It was the weirdest thing I had ever seen in my life. While at Towson, the university formed a Black Student Union to address some of the cultural complexities many of the students were experiencing. I will personally say, I did keep my hair story limited and conformed to a more straightened and relaxed look so that I could transition smoothly and graduate. By the time I graduated and began to look for job placement there was a piece of me missing again. I asked myself, who had I become? I will say the relaxed look provided me with more opportunities in the corporate world, but I felt like my true identity was missing. When I finally started working, I got a job with a federal government agency, and Towson requested I come back and serve as a panelist on the cultural diversity committee. It was this experience that challenged my own cultural identity the most. That day, as I prepared for the speaker's series, I just could not get my hair to act right in this relaxed state no matter how much I curled it. On that day, I was reminded of the press and curl days when my hair would revert back to its original state, and it hit me to my core. Then, I heard the moderator ask me, "How do you identify yourself?" and all I could say was, "I am Black!" Then there were a series of questions. I asked myself; Who are you really? That's when I started singing that song, "I am not my hair, but I am more than my hair…Yes, I am the soul that lives within." That's the day I began my transition to relaxer free hair, and it's been a journey. A powerful one.

11

Regal Hair

April S. McLamb

find it interesting that wearing natural hair is a trend now. I decided to wear my hair in its natural state back in 2008. I grew tired of having to spend countless hours in the hair salon chair waiting for the "creamy crack" to be slapped onto my head, while feeling the burning sensation, and then commence to spending at least an hour and a half under the hair dryer. One day a sister-friend I'd met in graduate school said, "Why don't you wear your hair natural, April?" I had NEVER considered this before that moment. A novel idea, it was intriguing yet had me feeling so scared, because I didn't know what this unchartered territory would be like. I thought to myself, "How will I look?" and "Is my face too fat?"and "What will my Momma say?" And the question I think that runs through every Black woman's head who is thinking about going natural, "Will men find me attractive?" I was in graduate school at a predominately white institution in New Orleans, Louisiana. During this time in my life, I did many things to please others. I was in my early twenties. It is my belief that in your early twenties you usually don't know what in the world you want to be, how you want to be, or how you want to present yourself to the world. So, I did what a lot of people do now, I conducted a Google Search and looked at women who would be my "go to" of how I wanted my hair to look after I went through the process of the "BIG CHOP," (cutting off all processed hair leaving only my natural hair). One picture came to my view and that was of the iconic, Angela Davis. I knew who she was and what she stood for, but there was something about this picture that made her appear to be regal, unrelentless, and beautiful. I named Ms. Davis my "hair shero!"

Next, I strategize about how I was going to grow my hair into a perfectly shaped afro. The journey…the process. Oh yes, there is a process to transitioning from permed hair to natural hair. There is the physical process, and then there is the emotional process. The physical process of growing my natural hair did not make me upset or discouraged. I believe what was discouraging was the emotional process of my hair changing, and how people responded to it, particularly other Black women.

I had finally finished graduate school by this time and started a new job at a social service agency as a social worker. I would say the demographic of the staff was about eighty percent Black, and eighty-five percent women. During this time in my life, I was very insecure and still trying to find my way about how I wanted to present my hair, but at this point, I had a full "Angela Davis" afro.

Unfortunately, a lot of people did not feel about my hair the same way I felt about my hair. I felt indignant and frustrated when people stared at me and my hair, particularly Black women. I just couldn't understand it. When I wore my afro picked out and shaped, I felt so proud because I was personifying that picture of Angela Davis looking regal, pristine, and powerful. However, when I walked around completing job duties at work I often felt powerless, a bit ashamed, and strange because I would get stares from the other Black women, and then I would get passive aggressive gestures from them like a raised fist or words like, "power to the people." It felt uncomfortable hearing other Black women say this because I didn't understand their context. I could only assume these actions were meant to belittle or reject my natural hairstyle. I often asked myself, "Were they pointing out how strange my hair looked, or were they jealous at the audacity of me to wear my hair in an afro?"

Once someone approached me and asked THE QUESTION, "So, why did you go natural?" You will never believe who asked me this—a Caucasian woman! I felt taken aback, but in a good way because she sincerely wanted to know. So I explained to her that my hair was a form of expression, and then she began to tell me she grew up in the seventies, and how she always wanted to wear her hair in an afro, but didn't realize as a kid that hair texture made her hair different from that of a Black woman. Further, this co-worker of mine told me that Black women from her understanding would wear their hair in an afro to decolonize and deconstruct society's idea of how beauty should look. This woman shared that in the seventies wearing an afro was a political statement. When I left that conversation with her, surprisingly, I felt empowered. I felt understood, and I felt noticed; which at the same time grieved me because a lot of Black women continued to make me feel less than because of my hair choices. I felt sad that most of the women at my job didn't allow themselves to cross the barrier and just simply ask me the question.

After that day, I resolved that I would never again apologize for how I chose to wear my hair. How I wear something on my body is okay because IT'S MY BODY! I was no longer going to allow other people's thoughts of me, or their indirect responses dictate how I wore my hair and how I carried myself. To this day, I continue to wear my natural hair. Since then, I have had many natural hairstyles, but again I do these styles because it goes back to how I felt while looking at that picture of Angela Davis. Now, I continually pick hairstyles that make me feel regal, unrelentless, and free.

12

I Am Not My Hair

Marlo R. Green

*M*y paternal great-grandmother, Anna Wilson, was mixed race. It is said that my paternal grandmother, and the woman who raised me, also named Anna (Ricketts), was the spitting image of her mother. Both Anna's laid claim to beautiful, thick, long-flowing tresses that would make most women sacrifice a limb. Prior to me, my grandmother Anna never focused on hair, she never had to. She had raised four boys and by the time I came into the picture, she had chopped off her tresses and was left with beautiful, silver wash and go hair that she lathered with a purple shampoo. For the first time in her life, Anna had to wash, style, and maintain, thick, kinky, hair. My hair.

When I was seven, Grandmom Anna and I began the hair journey together. Down a long, windy, scary road of weekly washes, presses and ear burns until the day she decided to relax my hair. That day, she read the box, I read the box and then we read it together. This was her first foray into relaxing anyone's hair, but she managed to relax my hair with little to no burns and I walked away with silky straight hair. So began my addiction to perms. I rocked the straight style, curling it every night with rollers – first hard then soft–and when I finally got a curling iron, I used it to curl my hair every day. It was the mid 1980's and music and television impacted the way I saw my hair. Denise Huxtable always had funky hairstyles, but it was always straighter and sleeker. When Salt 'n Pepa came out I even got a friend to put in a piece of reddish weave to complete my hip hop look. My relaxed hair served me well through junior and senior high school – except for that one picture that was post straightening comb pre relaxer. I still cringe whenever I see that picture of me with a nappy unkempt bang and "wanna be" curls.

My grandmother was not conscious of the messages she gave me about hair. Often when seeing other black people, I would hear her comment about their hair. She would say "hmph, why couldn't they just comb their hair" or "why are there so many nappy headed negros running around". The message I received was that straight hair was better and that natural kinky hair was unacceptable.

Throughout the nineties, the hairstyles of Black women on TV continued to be straight hair with the occasional, rare, braided style. Maxine Shaw, from Living Single showcased a different look for Black women. While I wanted to embrace my natural hair, I always lived in fear of my grandmother's stereotype of being considered that nappy-headed Negro.

I lived with these notions throughout my twenties.

In 2004 when I got pregnant with my twins, I embraced the anti-relaxer idea and stopped relaxing my hair. Little did I know I was on the first step of my natural hair journey. While I stopped relaxing my hair, I did not stop straightening it. Every morning I would get up and flat iron my hair. I developed a technique that allowed me to flat iron and curl together using my GHD flat iron. While I daily rocked cute "straight" styles, I was literally destroying my hair day by day.

As I progressed in my career, I felt it was vitally important to maintain a standard of what I thought a professional person looked like. In my mind, Claire Huxtable was the epitome of a professional Black Woman with straight or perfectly coiffed hair, being neatly attired in business clothes and the ability to code switch for vernacular. There was no freedom of expression through hair, even if that freedom of expression was just wearing your natural hair.

I never thought I would get to the point of my own self-acceptance where I would interview and begin working with my naturally curly locks. My curly-haired awakening came in 2017, when I found myself traveling almost non-stop for work and hair maintenance became harder. It was then that I decided to condition my hair every morning, forgo blow drying and wear it without straightening it.

In 2019, I was approached about interviewing for a job. I interviewed with straight hair, received the job, but started with my hair curly. From day one, they had to love the curly haired me. Every few months, I would go to get my hair trimmed, which usually left me with straightened hair. One morning, after my trim, I went to work and the CBO looked at me and said, "oh you did your hair." The comment caught me off guard. I did my hair every day, today it just happened to be straight. So many thoughts and waves of self-doubt ran through me. Was that the perception? That I did not "do" my hair? While at this same job, I had a conversation with a member of the board of directors, he told me he thought I could be great on the public speaking tour if I fixed this–pointing to my hair then pulling on his, to look more professional.

About six months into my employment with the above-mentioned company, I dealt with a white co-worker who walked up to another employee and physically pulled her hair to determine if her extensions were attached to her head. A lot of what I learned in this space confirmed everything my grandmother ever said, but it also gave me the courage to stand firm in my own hair journey. I suspended the white woman for the hair pull while coaching and counseling the Black employee who had been assaulted, but in the end she still quit. Despite the severe and stern warnings issued, this employee still felt the emotional repercussions of being the one who got her co-worker suspended.

Recently, I began working for another company. My boss, an amazing professional, Black woman wears braids and has one side of her hair shaved. She makes no apologies for it. It does not impact her work, nor does it impact the way her co-workers view her. I respect her stance to be herself and each day my courage grows in my quest to be myself. I am learning that I am not my hair, it is just a part of me. My hair does not make me who I am completely.

Recently, I shared with an older, white friend that I would be documenting my hair journey and she didn't understand why Black women hadn't taken a stand earlier and united around our hair. While I tried to explain the hair journey, the attitudes around needing to find a job vs. wearing natural hair, she still did not understand why we didn't just change it. Today more than ever, I am confident that we can change it, one curly strand, braid, and loc at a time.

13

Deeply Rooted

Lisa Marsh

When I think about my hair, many times, I feel traumatized, you see I have had hair issues it seems almost from birth. As a little girl, I would often be referred to as "Hey, little boy," since my hair was so short and I didn't get a figure until I had babies. I would also be called "Scalp June" by my little brothers. Hence, my hair relationship was always contentious for me.

My mom would press my hair with a hot comb in front of our stove to try to get it manageable, then it would be too thin at the ends, and too thick at the roots. The back of my hair was always short and refused to grow, this caused me a great deal of pain and trauma growing up.

I had two sisters who were younger than I, and both seemed to have a better texture, grade and length of hair. I was always the outcast in my family. From the one with the shortest least manageable hair, to the one who always seemed a little different, a little off cue. My mom would try to sooth me by saying I was her love child, but I felt like she was really saying, it's okay little bald-headed different girl, you gone be alright.

This was the time in my life where I also struggled with my belief in God, thinking that if there truly was a God, he would not allow us to live the way we had to. We moved every year or two, which meant having to gain new friends, and learning new schools. It was a nightmare for me to find friends that I thought would accept me and my terrible hair.

My mom wore wigs for most of her life and was never really too concerned about hair, she allowed us girls to begin combing our own hair around the time I got my first perm, in eight grade. I would comb, flip, and curl my hair and still at the end of the day, or the next day, my hair would look like I was a black scarecrow.

I began to believe that my entire life would be marred by having a string of bad hair days, augh. Mom would try again to smooth things over by adding in her fixes. She would say, do you want me to press it, or do you want me to perm it for you, or style it. Mom did have a way of making me feel better and I loved spending time with her while she did my hair, even if it would end up the same at the end of the day.

Mom was happy to stop combing our hair right when we started getting perms, and we were happy to have her stop, the small burns on my ears, neck and forehead were wounds of the war I had lost. The burn marks would last many days after getting my hair hot combed, and the press would only last a day or two, and it was back to kinky again. The good hair days never outweigh the trauma of getting my hair pressed.

I grew up with a complex about being bald-headed and different. This complex stuck with me throughout grammar school, high school, well into my college days and probably after that. In college I learned to deal with my hair, I wore perms from eight grade through college, even sometimes pressing the roots instead of perming the naps, so I would have a perm and still have to press my nappy roots, not fun.

BECOMING AN ADULT

After college, I joined the national guard and went to basic training. During my military time, women were to have our hair pulled back or up and not below the collars on our Basic Dress Uniform (BDU's). It was during this time that I met my first husband who didn't seem to care all that much about my tacky hair, he loved me just the way I was, nappy.

From that union I was blessed with two bouncing baby girls…..
Noooo. Now I was the one in charge of getting hair combed and keeping it manageable and growing, "oh Lord Why hast thou forsaken me!"

When my girls were little, I loved barrettes, and bows, but I would pull their hair tightly trying to keep it braided and neat. I now regret pulling my daughter's hair like that because now they do it to their daughters. I would like to see this vicious cycle stopped, especially knowing what I now know.

BEING MOMMY

As a young adult mom of two girls, instead of me having to comb my hair and my girl's hair daily, I braided everybody's hair. I would go months with the synthetic hair in my head wearing braids, washing them while still in my head or not washing them for at least a month, what was I thinking? I would finish braiding our hair, and we could not sleep for at least a week because our hair was so tight. I thought I was doing us a favor by keeping our hair braided and manageable, NOT! Ashley and Brittany, please forgive me, mommy just didn't know any better!

My oldest daughter, Ashley was about two years old when a tragic incident occurred that involved her hair. We were out shopping and one of her barrettes got stuck in between the holes in the shopping cart where she sat. She moved trying to release herself from the shopping car and suddenly the entire braid was ripped straight from her scalp.

I was mortified, traumatized. I think I cried harder than she did, because she stopped crying to watch me cry, then went back to her cheerful self as if nothing had happened. You would think that episode would have stopped me from braiding their hair so tight or putting in barrettes to make their hair look longer and fuller. Those barrettes caused my little ones to lose sleep many nights, I know this now because I watch my grand-daughters deal with the same issues, tossing their heads back and forth to try and get comfortable, crazy.

Not knowing any better, I continued torturing my daughters for years with tight styles, but was strictly against perms. I had seen the way perms thinned my hair out. I wanted better for them than perms, so I said absolutely no perms for my little ones.

When my daughters were very young, their dad and I divorced. He moved back to Texas and I remained in Illinois. They had very little interaction with their dad for about a year, then I decided to contact him so they could visit. It would give me a break over the summer and they could bond with him. They missed him terribly.

I tracked him down and packed up my sweet little ones to go visit their dad. I had mixed feelings about them visiting, but knew how much they loved and missed him and how exhausting it was being a single mom, so off they went.

Our little bundles of joy would continue visiting their dad in Texas for a few summers, but one particular summer when they were about to return home, their dad called to tell me he had given them perms. I was furious and needless to say, this trip was my girl's last summer visiting him. My relationship with my ex-husband had diminished terribly. I believe he did everything he could to piss me off, so I stopped tracking him down, contacting him or reaching out for our daughters to visit him.

I pray to continue to educate my daughters on hair issues and not just for their sake but for the sake of my granddaughters. Perhaps I can educate my grown daughters on hair and men at the same time, ohhh, now that requires prayer. Dear heavenly father, please let my life be a shining example for my daughters and let them not make the same mistakes that I have, and if they do Lord, allow them to lean on you for Grace and Mercy, Amen!

UNDERSTANDING MY HAIR

It is only after my daughters are now grown, have left home and have daughters of their own, do I take the time to understand my hair and actually take real care of it.

I was never a weave person; I wore weaves once or twice but that glue and thread did not work for me. I tried to like the glue especially when girlfriends would wear the weaves and seemingly change their personalities. I know ladies who are still wearing weaves. It's like they get addicted to extra hair. Many ladies even have nice hair, they just seem to like weaves or wigs.

I admire the weaves, and wigs the young girls wear now, especially the different colors. Their hair looks different every few weeks. They rock afro puffs one week, the next it's flowing down their back touching their butt, the blue, pink or even fuchsia colors are cute but not really practical for me. If I get to see my daughter's real hair every now and then I think how nice it is and that they could save themselves a whole lot of money, (they spend hundreds of dollars on their hair and then wonder why they can't pay their bills). I think my girls should just go natural like me, but they adamantly refuse, like it's a curse, prayerfully time and I will teach them better.

My first granddaughter, my Diva baby, and I have made a joke about going natural and having nappy hair. We have read books about being Happy Nappy, loving our hair, and often sing and dance to just being Happy Nappy, I can hear the tune right now! Love it!

GOING NATURAL

Going natural for me was like a revolution, I was making a statement, here I am world, like me or not, but my husband absolutely did not! My going natural has taken some time to grow on hubby.

He used to make comments like, "Please tell me you are not going outside like that," or "Why don't you just braid it up, or get a wig." One conversation involving our youngest son went like this:

"Ok, honey," I said. "I am almost ready to go, how are you all doing?" I asked. "We are good," my husband responded. When I departed from the bathroom, my husband and our youngest son took one look at my head and both asked in unison, "Ummm what are you going through with your hair." I stated, "I am going natural, tired of dealing with the braids, and perms drying out my hair, or taking hours to press and curl it. Nope, no more taking hours to blow dry, then flat iron, then try getting the roots straight."

As me and my diva granddaughter Amaya sing and dance; "We are Happy Nappy," but my fellas obviously didn't get the memo.

Both of my guy's, young and seasoned, were annoyed at the concept of me going out in public with my hair just, just … uhhh natural. We were already late for our outing so on this one occasion I gave in. I pulled out my small wig assortment. I chose one with my guy's animated help, and we were off. I felt defeated, but knowing this conversation was far from over, for the sake of temporary peace, I caved.

I felt defeated by my hair journey, not to mention my man's attitude about my natural hair. My husband has many opinions on what is best for me, and I believe most of his personality comes from him being an only child and having his way through most of life. "WE are going to work through this come hell or high water," I thought to myself, reflecting on what my mom used to say!

Over the next few months, I begin to get more comfortable with my natural hair. It became more versatile and I could use curly products to give it a wave. I could also blow dry, flat iron and press it if necessary, but not often because I discovered that heat changed my curl pattern, I could now wear my hair twisted or I could crochet it (which was my husband's preference). I learned about protective styles that help the hair look better, allowing it to breath and grow. I even learned to stop greasing my scalp and started applying moisturizing products directly to my hair, since my hair was very dry and brittle.

My husband then began to say I own too many hair products and I was taking over the entire bathroom with a wide variety of hair products. He and I began to have weekly if not daily conversations about where I was going with my hair and why my products consumed our bathroom. I was just trying to find out which products worked well and didn't dry out my hair.

Slowly I began to discover that my hair continued to break, no matter what I used. I kept getting these bald spots in different places, so I discussed this with a stylist. At this point, I had gone through at least three to four stylists trying to find one that was reasonably priced, accessible, pleasant and available. I needed a stylist who actually cared about hair.

I tried finding a stylist or beautician locally because I refuse to ever again have to drive forty-five minutes to Chicago, or wait hours (between three–five) just to get into the shop chair while the stylist's worked on three people's hair at the same time. No Thank you! I need someone who cared about my hair and not just about my money. I need a beautician who wanted to see their clients with a healthy head of hair and not just a stylist who only cared about how much money he or she could make.

I am again traumatized. Why is it so difficult to find a beautician who works on natural hair, who won't cut you bald, and doesn't cost your first born. When I finally found a beautician I liked, she recommended that I see a dermatologist. I found a dermatologist close to me and made an appointment to go see her.

In the meantime, I attend my oldest nephew's wedding wearing a white scarf. I had gone to a stylist earlier who stated my hair was too damaged to do anything with and she proceeded to cut it all off, without my permission. I couldn't even grab enough of it to braid…again traumatized! I vow never to allow anyone else to dictate that I needed a haircut. Really, shouldn't this be an ask when you are taking on a client, excuse me lady, would you like a haircut? Hell NO, I have a retirement party, wedding, etc. to attend, put them damned scissors down!

I finally got in to see the dermatologist. She was nice, young, and white. She wore gloves during my examination, yet really didn't touch my hair. Since this was my first time ever seeing a dermatologist, I just shrugged it off to standard operating procedure to not touch the patient. From her brief assessment, she decided that I needed to have a biopsy to determine the underlying issue.

I was sent to a clinic that tests for disorders. I waited on my results then made another appointment to see the dermatologist. The people at the clinic taking the biopsy were cold, uncaring and seemed to not notice that I was unhappy and unsure about this recommendation. Not one lab technician asked if I was okay, if I would like some water or even if I understood what the heck I was doing there! I was uncomfortable with the entire process. I felt like a fish out of water, but I also understood the need to find out what my hair issues were, so I proceeded.

SJOGREN'S SYNDROME

When the test results came in, I went back to see the nice, young, white dermatologist. She tells me that I have a condition called Sjogren's Syndrome, which is a disorder of the immune system. The symptoms of Sjogren's are dry eye, dry mouth, and dry scalp. Sjogren's is usually accompanied by other immune system disorders such as Rheumatoid Arthritis, which I also suffer with. I am also gluten-free, which can also be caused by an immune disorder called Celiac Disease. I accept the diagnosis.

The dermatologist stated that I could be placed on harsh medications but the side effects would be worse than the Sjogren's. She provided me with information to deal with the diagnosis, over the counter supplements, liquid prescriptions, and creams. After my consultation with the dermatologist I felt encouraged. Now if I could only keep it decent, keep it growing and moisturized, I may be able to do this hair thing, even if my husband was not quite convinced!

I used the hair creams, liquid prescriptions and even picked up the recommended eye drops, and mouthwash. My hair started to grow back and instead of braiding it, I began having it twisted and actually enjoyed the variety of styles that twists allowed. My hair and the Sjogren's Syndrome were doing ok while I was taking the recommended over the counter and prescription remedies. I thought that I was in the clear. My hair was growing back, so I stopped using the tedious products, around the same time, my latest beautician was becoming aloof, she would miss appointments, have me waiting for hours, and always had an excuse. She was a really nice younger stylist that I had grown fond of, but here we were again, back to the drawing board.

THE HAIR TRAUMA CONTINUES

After some time, I found another beautician. She was close, only fifteen minutes from my house. When I arrived for my appointment, I was the only client getting my hair done in my time slot. She was reasonably priced, pleasant and available when needed. I got into a nice rhythm of taking care of myself and getting my hair and nails done on the same day twice a month. I felt encouraged and like I was a pampered princess. I deserved this, I worked really hard and finally I could enjoy some of the fruits of my labor. Hubby was even happy with this new routine, he liked that I had nice manicured nails and my natural hair was growing on him, whew finally.

He took the time to remind me of my appointments, and even decided on some occasions to pay for my day of pampering. Now this new space I could really get with, hair done, nails done, everything done!

My new beautician seemed to really care about the condition, softness, and maintenance of my hair. She maintained my hair for about three months, then noticed it starting to shed. My beautician was concerned about my bald spots. She noticed the spots getting larger, and in different locations. My hair was also thinning and breaking, especially in the crown.

She was seeing a Black dermatologist and referred me to her. I had a hard time getting an appointment with Dr. Patterson who to me was a unicorn. Unicorn meaning, amazing, hard to find, and remarkable. Dr. Patterson was the first Black dermatologist that I had ever met. She was well groomed and wore her hair in twists or lock's. She wasn't afraid to look closely at my hair, put her fingers in it, gloved fingers of course, and to tell me what she thought the issue could be.

The beautician who referred me to Dr. Patterson thought I had a fungus on my scalp that was causing my hair to fall out. She had herself experienced hair loss and decided to cut her dreadlocks and start over with the growth process, since I had been there, done that, I decided to pass on that option.

CENTRAL CENTRIFUGAL CICATRICIAL ALOPECIA (CCCA)

Central Centrifugal Cicatricial Alopecia or CCCA only affects Black women over the age of thirty-five, and doctors aren't really certain why the hair loss happens. CCCA could occur because of past hot combining, perms, dyes, or just plain tight hairstyles, hair being pulled or bound. Oh wow, another issue that we female, minority chicks could really do without. CCCA is a disorder that causes inflammation and destruction of the hair follicles which can cause scarring and permanent hair loss. The best we can hope for is to receive treatments that stop the follicles from dying, and the hair from falling out. The treatment can include prescription scalp creams and injections directly into the scalp.

I left Dr. Patterson's office with a pamphlet, and after having a biopsy of the scalp to determine if I indeed had CCCA. I did mention the earlier diagnosis of Sjogren's to Dr. Patterson, she seemed unconvinced and wanted to wait for the biopsy results to be certain.

I read the pamphlet, looked up CCCA, it is said that many African American females experience this balding in the crown of our heads. This disorder does not affect any other race, and has been around for years. When researching further, I found that African American females have been known to live with our hair crown thinning and many of us never seek help. I find it strange that we have not been educated about CCCA, and only find out when it may be too late. I have read that many treatments for CCCA are not geared at regrowing the hair since the follicles die and make regrowth almost impossible.

I was anxious to hear my test results and to finally know what I must face in order to finally have a head full of healthy hair. I have been told that women's hair is our crown of glory, so why was mine such a challenge.

After my test results were returned, I was ready to begin this fight. I exercised, ate right (gluten-free diet) , took supplements and moved as much as possible. Could I really have both Sjogren's and CCCA? If so, let's get on with this hair battle, one I intend to win.

I have been telling others about my diagnosis to educate and get them to look at CCCA and also to spread the word. Some women were like oh that sounds like what I have, and do nothing to address the issue. I told my mother-in-law and she has an appointment with Dr. Patterson to determine if she has CCCA, she has been educating her friends who are all in their seventies.

I asked Dr. Patterson as she was injecting the prescription directly into my scalp and using a cotton ball to remove the blood (strange and scary). The most important piece of information that I could give others related to CCCA. Dr. Stavonnie Patterson said that we as women, should be kind to our hair, do not sacrifice beauty over healthy hair, if styles are tight, this affects scalp health, anything binding, tight especially when we get those tight bumps.... (ohhh, I hate those), they are NOT good for the health of our hair. Ok, ladies, these hard-pulling ponytails, or heavy braids, or even perms that burn the scalp can cause damage to the hair follicles that in time can cause major irreversible damage.

Dr. Patterson also says to strike a balance between beauty and health, and when you first notice issues flaring up, hair loss in spots, blemishes that won't go away, dry irritated hair, skin, nails.... GO SEEK HELP!

She states that we should be proud of our hair texture and not try to fit into someone else's vision of what is beautiful. Then teach our children to love their hair and essentially love themselves.

Could this be why my Diva baby and I read, sing and dance to Happy Nappy!

I could not have said it better myself. I hold Dr. Patterson in high regard and love that she is open with her information, has no issues in touching my scalp, holding me accountable for what I currently do to my hair and scalp and found the diagnosis of CCCA in its early stages, to try and save my hair.

She prescribed a cream, and began the injections after my first two initial visits, my hair has been responding wonderfully. Dr. Patterson even stated that she believes that I was misdiagnosed with the Sjogren's and probably don't even have it. Interesting!

I returned to my beautician and could hear the joy in her voice about the growth and health of my hair and scalp, she said it really does her heart good to see the treatments working. She is proud that I am following the advice of Dr. Patterson.

I absolutely agree with her, I can see the difference in my hair and I follow the strict recommendations of using the creams three times a week. I get the scalp injections every eight weeks and have read that this will last six months to a year and gradually be reduced until the hair is healthy, strong and beautiful on its own, just like me!

So here I am, in the prime of my life, I finally love who I am, who God made me to be, a queen. A chicka who has made it from working in federal law enforcement dealing with some pretty shady characters, to the proud owner of Ms. P's Gluten Free. I have a husband who is now good with my hair choices and has accepted that natural hair is a good thing, I think..lol, anyway he says he loves me. He is my rock and helps me take on the world and I thank God for him! P.S. even when his only child syndrome kicks in, pray for us yall!

I am a lady who has raised two daughters, went through a nasty divorce to marry again to a great guy. I have raised two lovely daughters, and now have two wonderful grand-daughters whom I will ensure to teach about having a full, beautiful, healthy head of hair, as the three of us sing, and dance to Happy Nappy!

I will continue to discuss my two different diagnoses with any female who is interested in learning from my trials, so they know the signs to look for if they experience hair loss or issues. I know for sure that CCCA can be hereditary, and am continuing to research it so that I can let my daughters, grand-daughter's and others know how it affects African-American women.

I have read that Sjogren's is not hereditary and want others to also research any diagnosis to ensure the treatment is correct and will work for them. I vow to teach all that I have learned about my hair, the pulling, the tight braids, the perms, hot-combs, and other related styles that affect the health of our hair.

I am bold, beautiful, and brilliant. A strapping grandma, a gracious wife, a proud and trusting mom, and a child of the Most-High. I will survive! I am absolutely grateful, thankful and blessed to be on this hair journey, to have learned all that I have, and to now be deeply rooted!

Stay blessed and healthy!

14

When The Rules Don't Come Naturally

Karissa C. Harris, LCSW

*A*s for me and my hair, I will maintain its natural style. I will embrace every coil, every ounce of its texture and every style I can uphold. Though I stand firm in this conviction today, it wasn't always like this. Growing up, I always thought that Black hair was everything and unique in its own way! A variety of trends that included braids, cornrows, straightened/hot combed hair, chemically relaxed hair, jheri curl, hair extensions and more. I grew up in New Orleans, Louisiana where I attended predominantly African American schools and hair trends didn't seem to be a concern until I moved to Monroe, Louisiana at the age of seven. I considered Monroe to be a very small town compared to New Orleans. Although some of the areas were predominantly African-American, I attended a school with a diverse student population. It was then that I learned that my hair and my culture were different. I can recall being in this town that was so unfamiliar with my hair cut short and my curls real tight...because I had a jheri curl. This is a memory that I would like to forget, but one that is a part of my hair journey. A journey I did not realize had so many rules. I mean, sure there's a right and a wrong way to do things. However, if your hair isn't trending with the times, conforming to corporate standards or perfected to what the majority deems sufficient, you soon learn that the hair rules do not come naturally.

HAIR RULE #1: IF YOUR HAIR DOESN'T TREND, YOU CAN'T SIT WITH US!

Before the Jheri Curl, my mom would straighten my hair with a hot comb. I would cringe at the sight of the chair by the stove with the comb placed on the burners. I absolutely hated to get my hair straightened because the steam and the heat were terrifying every single time. My mom decided that she was tired of chasing me down to the floor to keep my thick and shoulder length hair straightened. So, prior to moving, my mom put a chemical relaxer (perm) in my hair, which resulted in my hair falling out in various sections. The best option was to cut my hair short so that it'd be even and apply the Jheri Curl process. This would allow my hair to be curly and potentially grow back healthy. Of course, at the age of seven, I just thought this was a new and cute style, not knowing I would get snickers and giggles from my peers. At the time, no one else at my school had a Jheri Curl. I mean a few of my cousins and some of my older family members had it, but no one in my class. Some kids would joke about me possibly wearing the shower cap to sleep, which was definitely the case. It also didn't help that the curl activator had a smell and left stains on the collars of my shirts. Kids would often stare at me and sometimes whisper their jokes to each other before pointing. Though I still made friends and was sort of the teacher's favorite, I couldn't help but realize that I was different and not in a good way.

The ridicule came from all races, but more so my own. I felt as though this style resulted in judgements that I had no control over. As some days were better than others, the judgement did not feel good. I was very self-conscious about my hair and no matter how much I tried, I could not mask it or the smell. I would try to wear darker colors and shirts with lower cut collars to hide the staining. I even tried wearing the combs on the sides to create a mohawk or I'd gather it into a puff to create the look of a ponytail, but it never hid the obvious. I somewhat envied the other Black girls who wore prettier styles on either hot combed or relaxed hair. I would beg my mom to change my hair, but she would always say that it wasn't time. As I reflect, it seems I was coping with the style to make it my own until my dream would come true. Finally, during the summer and before I entered the 3rd grade, I got my perm! I would sling my hair non-stop, nearly getting whiplash. It was shoulder length and still very thick. On the first day of school, I felt like the ugly duckling turned swan. People who never said a word to me, in the previous school year, were now talking to me. I even had a few admirers sending notes like, "Do you like me? Circle yes or no." Needless to say, my confidence was on another level in the third grade. I even "lost my glasses" because I was feeling myself...knowing darn well, I couldn't see. I was cute though!

HAIR RULE #2: MAKE SURE YOUR HAIR COMPLIES WITH COMPANY STANDARDS.

I maintained chemically relaxed hair for the majority of my life. I would join in on the trends every now and then. My mom has been a braider all of my life, so I mostly wore braided styles and became her hair model, which also built clientele. I've worn the zig-zag braids, criss cross braids, with beads, gold or silver hair jewelry and more. Once I became a teenager, she allowed me to wear blonde and/or red blended braids. I still don't know why I couldn't wear those colors prior to then. I'm sure it had something to do with being "womanish." It's funny how the same colors of hair were a norm in other cultures, but more of a privilege to obtain on our own. When I entered the world of work at the age of sixteen, I witnessed restrictions on hairstyles that impacted our culture the most. For example, no hair jewelry, no hair colors other than "natural" colors and I can't recall if dreadlocks were prohibited, but I vaguely remember there were restrictions for the males, if not both male and female. Natural hair colors are considered to be: black, brown, blonde, white/gray and some rare reddish tones like auburn. However, because Black employees were commonly known to have black, brown or gray hair, I felt as though we needed approval to dye our hair blonde or auburn. Would you believe I also had to enforce these restrictions? I was a supervisor and onboarding trainer for new employees. I wish I used my position to advocate more for our rights, especially since this fight is still ongoing today. I admit I was afraid to speak up and even more afraid to lose my job.

I followed the "hair rules" of every employer thereafter. My understanding was that I had to maintain a certain look to secure my employment and uphold a look that was presentable in the eyes of those that I thought mattered. Hearing words like: nappy, kinky, bad hair vs good hair, b-bs (also known as nappy) and others, meant to me that people saw the real you. For years, I covered myself from head to toe in order to make everyone else comfortable around me. I thought it would help me obtain consideration for leading roles, simply because I met the company standards and conformed to what they deemed as appropriate for me.

When natural hair began to trend more in the Black culture, I listened and watched as it evolved. I always thought that I could never see myself "going natural." I was always told that my hair was too thick and it would be hard to maintain. While that has definitely been proven factual, I'm glad I chose to embrace my natural hair in June 2017. It had been fried, dyed and laid to the side too many times to count, which caused a lot of damage and breakage. Prior to my transition, it had to be cut into a pixie style, which I loved, but this was after being severely damaged yet again. Once I moved to Texas, I could not maintain it, and therefore it continued in an unhealthy state. While searching the latest trends and scrolling on social media, I discovered a hair commercial. This commercial praised the natural state of our hair and made reference to how our hair was unacceptable in the times before us. A beauty that could not be obtained or duplicated by any other. I can remember smiling and reflecting like….Yeah! My crown is beautifully created in God's image. Why should I perm and burn my scalp to conform to what society believes I should look like? I researched further and learned of additional damages that are caused by the consistent use of chemicals on the scalp. After much consideration, I allowed the chemicals to grow out and welcomed my own hair identity.

HAIR RULE #3: HAIR ACCEPTANCE MAY VARY IN MOST RELATIONSHIPS.

Here I was again, a new resident from another state and new employee of a very diverse organization. I must admit that I was afraid my new look would not be accepted by my new employer. It resembled the feelings I had at the age of seven. I observed various styles and trends that were not just embraced, but appreciated within this environment. Yet, I was still self-conscious. I feared the thoughts of my peers and questioned the professional acceptance of my superiors. I wondered whether I would appear professional enough for the role or if I would get the same stares and snickers as I did in my childhood. In addition, I thought my natural hair would be a deal breaker with any potential personal relationship partner. Most men seemed to be attracted to the women that wore the opposite of natural hairstyles. All of these things were a factor as to whether I was still pretty enough, professional and worthy of these relationships...both personal and professional. There were even days that I hated my own hair. It was either bushy, too dry, too short, too frizzy, too coily, not curly enough, etc. I went through tons of products, could not establish a relationship with an affordable stylist and I had no clue on how to care for it on my own. Many times, I've wanted to return to a perm, but I ignored the thoughts of not looking good enough for them, and I looked good enough for myself.

Hair Rule #4: Rules are ALWAYS subject to change.

I conformed to my own beauty, both inside and out. I became more knowledgeable about my hair and myself in the journey of accepting all that comes naturally. Though I am not a spokesperson, but could be, I encourage women to at least try it. Especially those who share similar experiences with hair loss, damage, over-processing, etc. I walked around far too long with unhealthy hair. The chemical processing made it look nice, but it covered up the true damage of my scalp and my hair's true identity. For some, a relaxer is easy maintenance like the times we endured the dreadful straightening combs. It is what works and it is still a part of our culture. For others, it can be damaging. When I asked my mother about her choices for my hair, one of the things she stated without much thought, was "you were cute with it straightened." My response was, "so, I wasn't cute without it?" Of course, that is not how she really felt, but it was the first response she provided. This is also the first thought of many.

We all have a story, but I believe our hair tells a story that may extend far beyond our understanding. The ongoing struggles to establish what's appropriate for black women seems to be a never-ending battle. The reality is, our hair is uniquely textured and way too versatile to fit in any set of standards. I proudly wear my crown and when it's crooked, I know there are many black women that will encourage and ensure it is worn with pride. I may even wear it pressed from time to time, because as my social media Aunt Tabitha Brown would say, "That's my business!" Although the hair rules didn't come naturally for me, my hair and

I have history. Since discovering its identity and building my own self-love, I now have a sense of freedom, peace and most of all... strength. I encourage you to be the exception to the rule when it comes to YOUR HAIR!

15

Just For Me

Jasmere Bradberry

*D*ear Black girl, you are beautiful just the way God made you, and don't let anybody tell you otherwise! Dear Black girl, you are fierce! Please know that, own that, and believe that!

Let me tell you how my journey to natural hair started. My mom thought my sister and I had beautiful hair. She didn't want to do anything to change or alter our hair pattern, but my mom wasn't very good at doing hair although she did the best she could. Her best was single box braids with a bunch of colorful beads on the ends. She didn't know how to cornrow or anything uninformed like that. Single box braids were our go-to hairstyle and she would redo them as they got old or frizzy.

We lived in a two-family house. My grandmother lived upstairs, and we lived downstairs. My grandmother was our landlord. One day my mom wasn't home and my grandmother decided to put a relaxer in my hair. I had no idea what she was doing. She said she had a surprise for me, so I got excited. I believe I was six or seven years old at the time. Too young to fully understand what was happening. I just knew that my grandmother had a surprise for me. She always helped my mom manage my hair by straightening it with a hot comb. I'm not sure why she wanted to switch from temporarily straightening my hair to something much more permanent and detrimental to our health.

As I sat down in the chair of my grandma's kitchen, she said to me "I can't wait to show you my surprise. You're going to love it; you're going to look so pretty," with such excitement. Her excitement made me feel happy. Me being six or seven years old, I was feeding off her energy, so I became anxious to know or see this surprise that was going to make me look so pretty. She pulled out a box with a cute little Black girl on it. The girl on the box was wearing colorful ball ponytail holders in her hair, which was jet-black with shiny curls. Just beautiful!

The print on the box read, *"Just For Me."* I watched as my grandmother mixed a little bottle of clear liquid inside a large tub of white stuff. After mixing the contents of the box, she began to put the tub of white stuff around my edges and throughout my hair. It stunk horribly! I mean it smelled so bad! At this point, I was very confused and nervous about this stuff she's putting in my hair. I just had a feeling that something wasn't right. I was wondering if it was mayonnaise, but it didn't smell like mayonnaise. Then it started to burn badly, but she told me it had to sit in my hair for a little bit longer. At this point my head felt like it was on fire! I wanted to scratch it out of my head or jump up out of the chair; anything to get this mess out of my head.

Apparently, she left the relaxer in my hair way too long and when she finally rinsed it out, all my hair around my edges came out along with the white concoction. Judging from the look on her face, I knew she'd messed up pretty bad and she didn't know how to fix it, or what to do. She didn't want to make me feel unpretty or make me panic, so she pretended like everything was fine. I had no edges, I was bald! My grandmother did something very wrong and she knew that my mother was going to be pissed when she got home and saw my hair. "She was in trouble now" my little mind thought.

I heard my mom enter the house from downstairs and walk up the stairs to get me, but my grandmother ran to stop her, trying to explain what had happened before she entered the room and saw me and the damage that had been done to my hair. I guess this was her way to justify her actions or to ease my mother's anger, but as soon as my mom saw me…she was livid! I mean she was mad! She was upset because she never had a desire to put a perm in her kid's hair. She knew how to manage our hair to the best of her abilities and our hair was thriving without any issues in its natural state.

Now that my hair was relaxed, I noticed that a lot of the little girls at school hair were straightened with relaxers too. So, after a while, I wanted to keep getting my hair relaxed. It was nice seeing my hair in a different state and feeling it hang down onto my shoulders. My mom wanted to grow it out, so she proceeded to find solutions on how to grow my hair back and manage it. Therefore, she asked our neighbor's teenage daughter across the street from us to braid my hair every three or four weeks with braiding hair extensions.

Her mom and my mom were good friends and they hung out a lot. The daughter always did a great job giving me unique/cute braiding looks for school. She was nice and became sort of like a mentor to me. She also taught me how to braid and how to add braiding hair extensions. My hair grew back fast after three months, but my mom wanted me to keep getting the braids because it freed up time from her doing my hair along with doing my sister's hair as well. I did what we now call a transition. I transitioned in the nineties from relaxed to natural. Therefore, my hair wasn't as straight anymore, and I wasn't happy about it. I missed my hair hanging down on my shoulders.

After six months or so my hair was fully grown back, but I didn't want to go back to the natural state of my hair. My mom no longer needed my hair to be braided up with extensions anymore, so I told her that I wanted to start getting relaxers like the little girls in school. You know, when you're a kid, you're a follower. You want to do what everyone else is doing, not knowing right from wrong. My mom said, "Are you sure?" Then she advised me that she didn't think it was a good idea and that my hair was fine the way that it was. I wanted this so I begged, and she gave in and said, "you will be getting your hair done professionally at the salon by a licensed hairstylist this time." She was not trying to have another incident happen that would result in me losing my hair again.

My mom took me to get my first professional relaxer done at a Dominican salon and from then on, I got my hair permed until I was twenty-five years old. As I grew older, I didn't get them as often, because I grew up in poverty and after a while, my mom couldn't afford it. I would go for a month or two without a touch-up. She touched up my hair at home when she could. The ghetto touch-ups, remember those? She probably wasn't even doing it right because she wasn't a professional. So, I've been pretty much transitioning on/off my whole life.

Recently, I asked my mom how she felt about her mother, my grandmother, putting a relaxer in my hair as a child without her permission. To this day my mom is still pissed, and she told me that she had a private conversation with my grandmother back then asking her why she did what she did. Per my mom, my grandmother said that she did it to help her manage my frizzy hair by getting the kinks and curls out. My mom said she cussed her out and told her my hair is kinky curly and she didn't need help managing it in that way.

My mom and my grandmother never had the best relationship and this situation didn't make it any better. My mom said she kept her distance from my grandmother for a while and barely spoke to her for a couple of weeks to a month. She made sure my grandmother didn't damage my little sister's hair like she damaged mine. My bad experience along with my mom and I protecting my little sister's hair worked out in the long scheme of things, as she's been growing out her dreads for eleven years and they are now down to her waist. She literally sits on her hair.

The thought process of becoming natural to completely stop getting a relaxer is a very mental and emotional one. You start to realize that the process is much deeper than hair, due to society's beauty standards and different stereotypes around Black women's hair. I never understood why people cared so much about what we do and why we do what we do to our hair on our heads. Like seriously, why are people outside of the Black community and some who are ignorant within the Black community so pressed and fascinated by what Black women do with their hair? Along my natural hair journey, I've realized that people are just curious and it's best to help educate them and understand things unknown or unfamiliar to them instead of getting offended or arguing with them.

From the ignorant comments to the weird questions, you'll hear it all throughout your natural hair journey and will probably hear some while relaxed too. Relaxed or natural, people have said and done some weird things. That's been my experience throughout my life with my hair due to the texture and length. So many people would ask me, "Is that your hair?" It's so rude and disrespectful for someone to tell you that hair that grows out of your head isn't yours. Accused of lying and being told your hair is a weave. I've even had a man come up to me and ask me if my hair was mine while walking in downtown Newark, NJ, and when I told him yes, he pulled my hair and ran off. Like, really?! Extremely immature and ignorant! All because of a stereotype of Black women not being able to grow long hair, and if we have long hair...it's assumed to be a weave. Where did this ignorant rumor or stereotype originate from?

I've always had a good length of hair, and while relaxed, I wore my hair out most of the time. It was easy to do when I had a consistent hairstylist tending to it while I was in high school. I went to high school in Concord, NC, and a family friend of my aunt and uncle owned a hair salon in Charlotte. She and her sister's had long beautiful hair. That's where I would mainly get the weave comments. Saying things such as, "Your hair is so long and healthy. It's so shiny, is it yours? It looks like it could be fake or a weave." Ridiculousness! My hair isn't long like Rapunzel or anything like that. It was like past my shoulders, landing at my bra strap with a healthy shine. At that point in my life, I had healthy relaxed hair.

I didn't do much to it. I've always been lazy with my hair when it came to the maintenance of it. Just washed and blow-dried every two weeks in between my hair appointments. Wrapped it at night, brushed it down, and put a headband on for school in the morning. Sometimes I would braid it straight back in cornrows like Uncle Snoop, while rocking my Tim's. Those were my tomboy days. Too bad it wasn't normal seeing a Black girl with that length of hair. The ignorance and brainwashing run deep back from slavery days dating back to the 1600s. Despite the large natural hair community and the numerous representations of Black women with long relaxed and natural hair we have now thanks to the invention of social media, ignorant stereotypes that still exist.

I'm currently thirty-four years old and have been fully natural without any relaxers or chemicals in my hair since 2014. A childhood friend of mine, who was also a licensed hairstylist convinced me to go natural back in 2011. Six years strong thanks to her. I'm grateful for my awakening. She and her sisters had recently gone natural at the time and did the big chop. She thought my hair was pretty and she didn't feel the need to keep putting relaxers in my hair. She asked me, "Why do you think you still need to get a relaxer?" When I thought about it, I had no real reason. I just kept making up excuses on why I needed to get them. Honestly, it was just all I knew. At that point, I had no clue what my natural hair looked like. I just didn't want to cut all my hair off. My little peanut head wouldn't look right without hair, I thought. That's when she explained transitioning to me and advised that I cut little by little off as the relaxer grew out. I agreed, so Fall of 2011 was my very last relaxer and she cut my hair into a nice layered Bob. It was the shortest my hair ever been!

She educated me on some natural hair products I could use to manage my natural hair, such as Cantu. I was a little knowledgeable about the transition method and some products to use while going natural or after the big chop. All my knowledge was obtained through watching many YouTube videos and the rise of the natural hair community. I stayed on YouTube! I watched different videos every day and became obsessed with learning how to transition and manage my natural hair. I would stumble upon people and channels such as Traycee Simmons, My Natural Hair Sistas, Naptural85, Cool Calm Curly, Jewellianna Palenica, Ivy Charlaine, OhGinelle, NaturallyCreole, and so many more over the past six years. The people and channels I named are OG's in the game. It's crazy because the natural hair community wasn't even big around the time I decided to transition into natural hair. The community has come such a long way, with more growth to come.

Thanks to these brave and confident women sharing their natural hair journeys for the world to see. Many of us have learned how to care for our hair without going to the hair salon and saved lots of money doing so. I used to go to the Dominican hair salons because they were cheap, but you get what you pay for because all they ever wanted to do was perm my hair to death, burn it to death with hot tools, or cut it all off. All I heard was "Mommy you need a trim," every time I sat in their chair. I never got my ends trimmed so much in my life. They were very scissor happy! Many of them also had no clue on how to properly treat or care for natural hair.

I was young and dumb and used to let them do it too, shaking my head. It wasn't a big deal to me at the time, because my hair grew back so fast. As I got older and started to educate myself on natural hair care and hair growth with all those YouTube videos, I wasn't beat for no mess! I stopped going to those non-licensed, lack of knowledge hair stylists. I went to my trusted child-hood friend when I needed help, the one who started me on my natural hair journey. She cared about the health of my hair. Messing around with those other hairstylists, I stayed stagnant at shoulder-length for a while. Now the only time you'll catch me in a salon is to get my hair braided up with extensions by the Africans for a protective style. After gaining enough knowledge from YouTube, I stopped letting anyone touch my hair outside of myself and I was able to grow my hair back to bra strap length close to waist length at times.

I was saving money from going to the hair salon and hair stylists but spending the saved coins up on hair products. By watching all these YouTube videos, and learning how to style and manage my natural hair, I became a product junkie. I was buying a new hair product every week and subscribing to the monthly product subscription CurlBox. It was ridiculous! I was trying to buy everything the ladies on YouTube used in hopes it would work on my hair. I was waking up super early to do my hair before work. Documenting my hair with pictures and stuff. I became obsessed with natural hair care.

I ended my transition almost three years from the date I started, trying to hold on to those dead ends. I started my natural hair journey in the Fall of 2011, and I was finally cutting the last bit of my relaxed ends off in the Spring of 2014. I am still going strong without wanting to run back to a perm, but it has not been an easy journey. It's a struggle managing natural hair, and it can be very time-consuming. Over the years, I've become a "lazy natural" and managed to make my life much easier and cut my long wash days down to an hour. It took many years of educating myself on my natural hair; from the curly pattern, the density, the porosity, scalp health, best products for your hair type, and natural hairstyle and techniques that work best for your hair and lifestyle. Everything I've mentioned is extremely important, but scalp health is the most important key to growing healthy hair from your roots.

The products you use can have a positive or negative effect on your scalp. Since becoming natural, I have developed scalp psoriasis. I'm still learning how to manage that. So far, I've learned that washing my hair every two weeks doesn't work well for me and I must clarify my scalp with a sulfate-free shampoo. I try my best to wash my hair every week, but I'm lazy and ain't nobody got time for that! I'm so lazy that I wear wigs as a protective style more than anything now. Wigs are the best thing since sliced bread! They are fast and easy, especially when you're trying to get ready in the mornings. I can switch up my look when I get bored and not worry about damaging my natural hair.

Since I'm a lazy natural, bun hairstyles are my go to when I am giving my hair a break from the wigs and braid extensions. You can thank my little sister for putting me up on the wig game. She grew her beautiful long dreads under wigs for a couple of years until she had some length. Nobody knew she had dreads under there, but me and her close friends. When I started my natural hair journey, my go-to styles were roller sets, perm rods set, and twist outs. I imitated my girl TheNotoriosKia from YouTube signature afro, where she would wash her hair, blow-dry, flat twist it, and roll the ends up with small perm rods. Part across the middle of your head from ear to ear, then flat twist your hair down in the front towards your face. Then flat twist the back down your neck and back. Halfway down each twist, add a perm rod on the end of your hair. I would do this at night and sleep with a satin scarf or bonnet over my head until the next morning. If your hair is thick then I suggest you sit under a bonnet hair dryer.

Once I took it down in the morning, I had a gorgeous curly afro. So powerful and beautiful! That fro was just for me, yes indeed! The key to taking it down is making sure your hair is fully dry, slowly taking apart your twists with oil on your hands to avoid frizz, separating and picking your twists out, but not too much because you want it to look fresh and last for a week. My hair was flourishing from that go-to hairstyle. Growing like weeds and looking thick and healthy. I did this style while I was transitioning and it made it easy to manage that line of demarcation while making those relaxed ends fade away quickly.

A bit of advice to my new naturals who plan on transitioning; don't expect your hair to look like the women you see on YouTube. Everyone's curl pattern is different, and your curl pattern will be different from when you transitioned to when you are fully natural. I don't want you all to be disappointed with the curls growing out of your head and what God gave you like I was. I thought I was going to have a looser curl pattern. Nice little spiral curls or something like that, but nope! That was not the case for me at all. Let me tell you, my hair is kinky, curly and it shrinks a lot. Shrinks right up on my head having you think I had no length at all. I could not believe it at first!

It took me some time to wear my natural hair out. I had no confidence whatsoever on how to wear my hair. What was I going to do with it? How was I going to style it? It was not looking the same as the girls I learned from over the years on YouTube. I couldn't see any length and I hadn't even cut that much. I probably cut off maybe three to four inches of relaxed hair and it looked like I cut so much more off. This was the hair God gave me. I had to realize that it shrinks up, meanwhile I was embarrassed to step outside. One day, something told me to just DO IT! I don't know what it was, but my confidence came out that day and I went to work with my hair in its natural state. I was so self-conscious about what everyone else was going to think.

In 2014, I worked at a law firm at the time. It was a very diverse work environment with people of all different backgrounds and ethnicities. It wasn't so bad. The guy I was dating at the time, he was so supportive. He said, "You look beautiful." He loved my natural hair, and it made me feel so good. He called me beautiful every day. I also got compliments from other ladies at work. I rocked it! My coworkers and boyfriend gave me validation and support, which is key during your natural hair journey. He took a picture of me outside beside my car with my shriveled-up hair. I loved it and every day after that, I fell in love with my natural hair.

Over the years while working in Corporate America, I've gotten so many compliments from other races and other Black women. They'd say, "Oh my God, your hair is so beautiful" and then try to touch my hair. "Look, but don't touch!" You can not be afraid to let people know not to touch your hair. Like I mentioned earlier, you will get a lot of questions from other people about your natural hair. They're curious and want to understand. Just stay calm and educate them. You will be asked questions such as, "What products do you use? How do you get your hair to stay up like that?" etc. Why not help another Black man or woman to learn about their natural hair and become liberated? People of other races will also ask you a bunch of questions. They don't have Black hair, but want to understand Black hair care practices. Some are asking because they have mixed kids at home and need help styling or managing their hair. Help educate them if they are genuinely asking without being racist or disrespectful.

There are times where you'll feel the tension when you walk in a room or area and your hair will make people uncomfortable. Your style, preference, or choice will make people uncomfortable. I would get them when I would wear faux locs, a curly afro, or afro puffs. I did receive compliments from Caucasian women from time to time, but I also received ignorant comments as well. For example, I was wearing a black straight wig one day at work and my manager said to me, "Oh my God, your hair looks so nice like that. You should wear your hair like that all the time". To stay professional, I said "thank you", but after some thinking about her "compliment" later that day I was a little bit offended. Like, what was that supposed to mean? This is what I call a backhanded compliment, but fortunately, I was now confident with my natural hair, but due to that backhanded ignorant comment, I switched up my hairstyle and the next day they got a natural afro puff!

Our hair is super versatile, where we can switch it up any way we like. Therefore, I switch up my hairstyles every two to three weeks. I love the versatility. I'm proud of it! I get bored sometimes, and besides, who wants to have the same hairstyle every day? No ma'am, not me. I have a love/hate relationship with my hair but love my corkscrew kind of curl pattern now. My curls aren't uniformed, and it can't hold a curl for anything, but I still love it! I use products to help me get curls and spirals, like mousse, certain gels, or curling custards. Sometimes I get a curl and sometimes I get a wave. Even when my hair was relaxed, it couldn't hold a curl for my life. The wind would blow them right out. I have a zig zag/corkscrew natural curl pattern and I get so many compliments on my hair.

There you have it, my natural hair story. Every day is a struggle, but I wouldn't want it any other way. I love my hair and wouldn't trade this journey for anything in the world. To anyone with a desire to go natural, just do it! I wouldn't advise transitioning as I did. The natural hair community was just getting popular and wasn't as big as it is now, and I wish I would have started my natural hair journey with a big chop. Don't keep waiting, just do it already and be free. You'll be doing yourself a disservice if you stall or wait. Free yourself, liberate yourself! Rock that afro, twist out or braid out! Be bold, be beautiful. Black hair is Queen!

16

Breaking Free:
Establishing New Roots To Freedom

Phyllis C. Cross

My name is Phyllis and I am a fifty-one year old college graduate, sister, daughter, caregiver, confidant, friend and I am a current graduate student at The Chicago School of Professional Psychology finishing my Master's degree in Clinical Mental Health Counseling. I am also a former convicted felon and a recovering addict. I did not share that information for shock value, I shared it because it is the truth. We cannot heal what we do not acknowledge. I know, I hear it all the time- that looks can be deceiving, or that "You sure don't look like what you've been through" (*Insert a praise break!!*). You are correct, and I know that it is the way that God intended for it to be. I am blessed- better than blessed, and I know it. I am humbled by it. I rejoice in it. I receive it. Let me tell you a story about hair and its impact on our lives. So, get comfortable, go and grab a blanket, your favorite beverage, and let's get into it!

Who remembers Saturday mornings getting your hair washed, pressed, and combed or braided while Soul Train was on? If you sat still, we would be through in no time, but if you moved and played around- you would get popped with the comb! Yes, me too. My struggles with hair started at a young age as with any young woman who is coming of age. My mother styled my hair in the usual ponytail, sometimes with bangs as a young girl, and as I got older, I could wear it down on special occasions. Those were the good old days.

As a teen, I grew up wanting to be just like my friends in the neighborhood and wanting to emulate the styles that we were exposed to on television, in magazines, and in movies. We grew up in the eighties, so who did not want the "Salt-n-Pepa" long/short combo with bamboo earrings, or the finger wave, or braid styles? I cannot think of one person who did not want that kind of acknowledgement. I have rocked everything from braids, perms, weaves, Jheri Curls, wigs, and everything in between and was still not happy nor satisfied with myself. Hair is supposed to be a woman's crown and glory, but what if she doesn't have anything else to offer but her hair and looks?

If you have it all, consider yourself blessed, but what about those women whose self-esteem and confidence lies in their looks? Have you ever thought about that on a deeper level? Seriously, think about it. Are all that you have to offer are your hair and your looks? Sweetie, if all that you have to offer to your-self and your future significant other are Gucci bags, a truckload of makeup, too little outfits, waist trainers, and other ridiculous apparatus that keeps you from being your authentic self, please sit down somewhere because you are missing the point. Do yourself a favor and go find you some integrity, perseverance, grit, hustle, and tenacity. No shade- just truth.

I needed a sense of belonging early in life and styling my hair in different ways allowed me to "fit in" with the crowd. See, I have always been the chubby girl, the "homegirl," the "cool friend," and my hair was a way to establish and solidify my place in that world. Their world, not mine. What was "their" world, you ask? It was a place of always trying to keep up with what others were doing, a place of feeling inferior to those around you, and to be accepted, it was normal to conform. It was a toxic place, not safe for a teenager trying to find their place in the world. It bore harsh words, glaring stares, silent whispers, and pointed fingers. It was the perfect storm for a girl who already felt insecure in this world. A place she did not belong. This world was shallow, and she had more to her than that.

As I began to make bad decisions in my late teen years and young adult life, my hairstyles reflected the way that I was living and the people that I chose to hang around and associate myself with. My style would depend on who I was involved with and what they wanted, instead of what I wanted and how I felt about myself. I would wear weaves, even though I disliked them. Don't get me wrong, they can be beautiful on some people, but they were not for me. I always felt tied down, trying too hard, wanting to be someone other than myself, and trying to portray an image that was nothing like me at all. I was seeking approval and validation and having my hair a certain way created that illusion for me, at least in my mind.

One time, I had a boyfriend that always complimented his ex-girlfriends' hair, her style, and everything in an attempt to make me feel jealous and bad about myself. I know now that he had control issues and that he tried to hurt me on purpose. Of course, in an effort to please him, I spent hundreds of dollars on different styles, wigs, braids, weaves, wasted Saturdays in a salon, and countless valuable hours that could have been used doing something productive and fulfilling. Guess what, he hated them all and he made no mistake in telling me that he did. His words crushed me and fractured my already fragile self-esteem.

Well, fast forward several years later, I ran into the same guy at a store in the neighborhood that I grew up in, missing some teeth, begging, looking ragged, and he had the audacity to tell me how good it was to see me and that I was looking good these days. What he did not know was that I already knew that and no longer needed or cared for his approval. I will admit, for a moment I almost felt sorry for him and on the other hand, I felt relieved to have finally gotten the unspoken apology that I needed for so long to be free.

What I know now is that I really do not care what others think of me or my hair. It is my choice and my prerogative to wear what I want and wear it the way I like, embrace my features that I forgot that I had, and walk in a certain confidence that no one else can give me. I love my hair and I love the woman who is wearing it. I have gotten more compliments than I have ever expected, but not surprised at the people who still question why I don't choose to wear my hair in the latest style, braids, or lace front wig. Been there, done that! I choose a close cut and on the days that I feel like I want to grow it out a little longer, then I choose that. Whatever makes me happy and brightens my spirit is the style that I choose, and I go with the flow.

My decision to cut off my hair happened after years of breakage, bad perms, indecisiveness, unhealthy edges, bad hair days, and being uncomfortable with the way I looked. It happened in July 2014. I took a long lunch break, went to the barber shop armed with the recommendation of a close friend and had it chopped off, cut with trimmers and razor edged to perfection. The barber, affectionately known as JD to his customers, has been my barber ever since. We have had many conversations about women and short hair. He is supportive, kind, funny, and excellent at what he does. The moment he ran the clippers through my head, it was like someone was setting me free. I immediately felt like years' worth of burdens had been lifted from me. At first, I was ashamed and thinking, "What in the world have I done?" and "Oh God, I look like a boy!" Then the negative thoughts emerged one by one... "My mother is going to think I have lost my mind or going through a midlife crisis," and "Someone is going to think I'm having a mental health breakdown," "This is not going to be acceptable at work," and/or "Who is going to want to date or marry you with your hair like that?" You know what, who cares?

Several thoughts have crossed my mind over the years about dating and marriage later in life. Do men love women with long hair? Is long hair and salon appointments a prerequisite, a deal-breaker, a topic of discussion, or an argument waiting to happen? At my age, that does not matter to me either. The decision is made. I will rock my short, cropped, colored, low cut, barber shop every two-three-week hairstyle, as long as it suits me; single, dating, married, or not. I know for sure that it will take a secure man, a confident man, a man that knows what he wants to handle the light and love of a grown, confident woman. I have earned the right in my life to do whatever makes me happy, including choosing the hairstyle that I love. I no longer aspire to be liked by anyone, because anyone who is in contact with me knows that my smile, my personality, and my spirit are contagious, hair or not! I am content, happy, joyful, blessed, and free.

My mindset became set in stone about my decision to cut my hair while in the bank one day taking care of some business. I am standing in line and a FINE brother, ladies I mean *Fine, Fine*, chocolate, well-groomed, smelling good and casually dressed complimented me on my fresh haircut and color and that did it for me! I was feeling myself after that. You couldn't tell me nothing! That gentleman affirmed me, and I didn't have to code switch, perform, change my voice or my persona. All I did that day was show up as my authentic self: *Beautiful, Bold, and Black.* It was at that moment that I had an epiphany- that all I had to do was show up authentically and I would attract the right people with the right energy into my life.

After that spiritual epiphany, things started happening in my life that I had been praying for over many years. God said it was time. I followed HIS lead. HE said, "Take your life back, Phyllis!" and I did exactly that. I was able to grasp and hold onto a level of courage that I never thought I had, and I got busy working. Freedom allows you to live in your truth, tackle the hard things, do the work, and change your life. Freedom allows you to be brave, fearless, amazingly strong, secure in yourself to do the things that you thought were impossible, and it was more than just a haircut. I needed to change my victim mentality, my thoughts about myself, my attitude, my look, and take my life back that I had given to others shamefully, unknowingly, and willingly at times. It was not theirs. It was mine and I wanted it back. I took it back, one mistake at a time, one bad decision at a time, one failed relationship at a time, slowly building and enjoying the life that I desire and deserve, and I have been living happy, content, and free ever since.

The more compliments I received, the more I embraced this new me! I seized the moment and found pretty shades of lip glosses, started buying different types of sunglasses, bought beautiful pairs of earrings and other accessories, perfected my smile, straightened my crown, and kept it moving! I am so glad that I did. I would have missed out on the beautiful person that I am emerging into.

You see, cutting my hair provided me with freedom in so many ways- freedom from bondage of the thoughts and opinions of others, freedom from the negativity that I had been carrying around for so many years, freedom from toxic relationships, freedom from the mistakes that I made, freedom from the regrets that I have lived with, freedom from unrealistic expectations of others and myself, and freedom of the lie that beauty looks a certain way and is defined by societal norms. I made the decision that day in the bank to establish new roots for me to continue to grow into a healthy, secure, and confident woman. I shared my story with you to say this:

DEAR BEAUTIFUL BROWN GIRL,

Sis, you are beautiful just the way you are! Stop trying to be someone that you are not. Embrace all of who you are- good, bag, ugly and indifferent. Trust me: let go of your past, forgive, and move on, go back to school, finish that degree, start a business, take care of yourself and do what makes you happy. Establish new roots. Water, nurture, let the light in and allow God to do what HE does. Stop allowing naysayers, haters, and followers to dictate how you feel about your look or your life. Free yourself- whatever that looks like for you. For me, it was with my hair and my style. Go ahead; change your look, wear a wig, get dreads, cut it off, go natural, rock your coils, braids, shaved, color, straight, long, short or bald! Whatever you decide to do, do it with con- viction, do it with boldness, standing in courage and in truth and I promise that you will not regret it! Go ahead. You know you want to, and you deserve it! Blessings to you and the journey that you choose.

Peace, Love and Hair Grease

Conclusion

$\mathcal{L}$et's put an end to the unspoken hair myths that have haunted generations of Black women, while remembering there is no such thing as bad hair. Just because your tresses may not resemble the woman to your left or your right, does not mean that you are imperfect. Made in God's image, Black hair no matter the texture, color, style or length should be celebrated. Now is the time that we must collectively come together and begin to talk about the hurts and pains that society has imposed on us because of our uniqueness which is a part of our Blackness. Let's move past the aftermath and how we have allowed others to contextualize kinky, curly hair as being "not good enough."

Rise up Black woman, rise up! It is time that we stop the bullying of Black women both within and outside of our race. Yes, we have the CROWN Act on the horizon, but as we all know, it takes more than a simple law to change the attitude and mindset of a nation. We must work together to end the internal oppression and struggles that many of our young Black women face. We must stop those within our race who continue to perpetuate colorism, sexism and self hate. The torch has been passed to you and me. It is our responsibility to build up a generation of little Black girls, teaching them how to love who they are, hair texture and all.

As a people, let's stop conforming to standards that were never meant to help us, but only hurt us. We are all Black and our uniqueness is that there isn't a carbon copy. No two Black women look the same and that's a beautiful thing. Together let's forge new paths that allow us to embrace the braids of our ancestors, the afro of Angela Davis, and the wigs, perms and weaves of Beyonce. Black hair is a part of Black beauty and everything about our beauty is flawless!

If you enjoyed reading this anthology, please share a copy with your family, female friends and even your book club. We'd also appreciate it if you would leave a review for *Can't Tell Me Nothing* on Amazon and Goodreads.

Don't forget to grab a copy of our sister anthology, Shut'em Down: Black Women, Racism and Corporate America.

Dr. Carey Yazeed

Made in the USA
Coppell, TX
24 February 2021